MW00605765

Building Community:
Defining, Designing, Developing UniverCity

An Ecotone Publishing Book/2018
Copyright ©2018 by Gordon Harris

Ecotone Publishing is an Imprint of the International Living Future Institute

For more information write:

Ecotone Publishing
1501 East Madison Street Suite 150,
Seattle 98122

Authors: Gordon Harris with Richard Littlemore
Book Design: Johanna Björk / softfirm
Edited by: Fred McLennan

Library of Congress Control Number: 2018937774

Library of Congress Cataloging-in Publication Data
ISBN: 978-0-9972368-4-2

1. Urban Planning   2. Design   3. Sustainability   4. Business

First Edition

Printed in Canada on FSC-certified paper, processed Chlorine-Free, using vegetable-based ink.

FSC
www.fsc.org
MIX
Paper from
responsible sources
FSC® C016245

CONTENTS

UniverCity

ACKNOWLEDGEMENTS

While it is a great pleasure to celebrate the emergence of UniverCity as a complete and resilient community, we could never have built this project — or told this story — without the inspiration, energy, brilliance, and determination of a grand cast of characters.

I have to begin by acknowledging John Stubbs who, as president of Simon Fraser University in the mid-1990s, had the insight and the resolve to give life to a longstanding good idea — the building of a community on Burnaby Mountain to complement SFU. The university and the UniverCity project were both lucky in the years that followed to enjoy the strong and constant leaderships of subsequent SFU presidents, Jack Blaney, Michael Stevenson, and Andrew Petter. It is no accident that SFU emerged in this period as the most celebrated comprehensive university in Canada.

SFU Community Trust is deeply indebted to founding Chair David Gillanders. A brilliant lawyer and a rock-steady hand, David's wisdom and guidance was foundational in the early stages and crucial through the whole 17 years of his service. He helped recruit, and presided over, a Board of Directors that has included a who's who of the Vancouver business and development communities. We have, at all times, been well-advised.

It would also be difficult to give adequate credit to Michael Geller, the first President and CEO of SFU Community Trust. An architect, planner, real estate consultant and developer in his own right, Geller was inspired and entrepreneurial, bold enough to be experimental and smart enough to recruit and connect with some of the region's most reliable developers. At a time when some people wondered whether UniverCity would get off the ground at all, Geller insured that it was soaring in no time.

I'd like to offer significant personal acknowledgement and profound thanks to two people who, regrettably, are no longer with us to hear it. The first is my friend Warren Gill, a remarkable urban geographer and professor at SFU, who is perhaps best remembered for his contribution to establishing the university's downtown Vancouver campus. But his advice about UniverCity was always invaluable, as was his personal support and encouragement. Also on this list — and unforgettable in every way — is the redoubtable Pat Hibbitts, the former Vice President Finance at SFU and consistently one of the wisest, wiliest, fiercest, and funniest members of the SFU Community Trust Board of Directors, and a dear friend. There were dozens of occasions when the diverging priorities between SFU and UniverCity might have created a critical conflict or restricted the scope of the Trust's ambition — but never with Pat in the room. She was a woman who saw only solutions and I feel privileged to have benefited so much from her energy and good will. Warren Gill and Pat Hibbitts: both are sorely missed.

There are many others to credit for building the community and helping with this book — not least the Trust's Vice President of Development Dale Mikkelsen and Controller Suzan Fairfield, along with other past and current members of the SFU Community Trust team. This book would not exist without the organizational brilliance and persistence of Pansy Hui, the Trust's Manager of Communications and Community Relations.

I will close by acknowledging my writing partner, Richard Littlemore, whose eloquence, skill, patience, and good humour helped bring this story to life.

GORDON HARRIS, 2018

Harmony at UniverCity.

FOREWORD
BY ANNE GIARDINI, OC, QC, SFU CHANCELLOR

It can't be by chance that the foundational stories of enduring societies begin with the creation of a place where people can live together. However the land, sky and oceans are made, whether by god, fox, raven or turtle, origin tales are visions of possibility and abundance, teeming with animals, plants, trees, water, warmth and light. These first imagined places are suffused with the premise that humans may in an ideal world be able to live in harmony with nature and with others.

Few planners have the opportunity to create a community from idea to full realization, and of those who have done so, many seem to have ended up with something very far from the ideal.

Scale seems to be important for getting it right. Christopher Alexander, Sara Ishikawa, and Murray Silverstein in their still-influential 1977 book *A Pattern Language*, write of the merits of a population of 7,000 or so, arguing for

> ... communities of 5,000 to 10,000 persons. As nearly as possible, use natural geographic and historical boundaries to mark these communities. Give each community the power to initiate, decide, and execute the affairs that concern it closely; land use, housing, maintenance, streets, parks, police, schooling, welfare, neighborhood services.

UniverCity, a built neighbourhood that is both part of Simon Fraser University and a thriving entity in its own right, has now reached this scale, and the people who live here today seem to be thriving in many of the ways that the authors of *A Pattern Language* envisioned.

Residents of UniverCity benefit from a neighbourhood that is both distinctly theirs and also connected both visibly and invisibly to the University, the City of Burnaby, and the surrounding greater Vancouver area. The people who call UniverCity home benefit daily from the commitment to sustainability and liveability of the many planners and builders who have created this place, whose stories are told in this book. The carefulness with which their community has been realized is observable to even the most casual eye. On closer inspection, the thought and attention to detail is astonishing.

In my roles as Chancellor of Simon Fraser University, as a past Governor of Simon Fraser University, and as a past member of the board that has oversight for UniverCity, I find myself at the top of Burnaby Mountain often. I never fail to pause, to take time to admire the way this community's streets flow fluidly in and over the contours of the mountain, the quality, diversity and verve of the homes and other buildings, and the sometimes verging on irreverent sense of fun in the design of the public art and amenities of this remarkable place. Visitors who walk through the streets and paths here quickly get a sense of the experimental joy that underlies how this place has been brought into being, grounded as it is in deep knowledge about the ways in which people truly wish to live, and in an abiding respect for the land and air and water we share.

From above, the shape of UniverCity reminds me of Bill Reid's famous carving showing the Haida myth of Raven discovering the first men inside a clamshell. On foot, the community feels open, safe and welcoming. It encourages discovery on foot. In our West Coast rainforest landscape, dominated as it is by dense green foliage under vast grey clouds, the buildings here provide contrasts of size, form, materials and colour. The homes of the residents are both grounded and aspirational. Their foundations are solidly set into the sturdy rock, while their large windows offer expansive views.

William Morris said, "Have nothing in your houses that you do not know to be useful, or believe to be beautiful." As a practical and beautiful setting to call home, UniverCity easily meets Morris's test. It provides a stress-free place to live and also a purposeful place, where residents are able to live well while drawing more lightly on the finite resources we all rely on.

The UniverCity residents I envy most are the pre-schoolers and elementary students. If I had it to do over and had any say in the matter, I would want to have lived and learned as a child here

Recognition has followed, among them a 2015 International Living Future Institute Living Building Hero Award, a 2013 Canadian Society Landscape Architects Award of Excellence for the UniverCity Childcare Centre, a 2012 Urban Development Institute Award for Excellence in Urban Development Best Sustainable for UniverCity Childcare Centre, a 2011 Canadian Institute of Planners Award for Planning Excellence: Neighbourhood Planning, a 2011 Federation of Canadian Municipalities Sustainable Communities Award for Integrated Neighbourhood Development, a 2009 Urban Land Institute Award for Excellence: The Americas for Best Practice in Design, Architecture and Development, a 2008 American Planning Association National Excellence Award for Innovation in Green Community Planning, a 2007 Urban Development Institute Award for Innovations in Creating a More Liveable & Sustainable Region, a 2006 Planning Institute of British Columbia Award of Excellence for Site Planning and Design, a 2005 Canadian Home Builders' Association SAM Award for Best Community Development in Canada, and too many others to list.

This book is a keeper. Make room for it on your shelf. Remember to take it down regularly to be reminded of the valuable insights in its pages as well as the hard-earned cautions. You will find humour in these pages, as well as home truths, how-to's and what-not-to do's.

This book is a valuable reference for anyone who cares about communities, that is to say, for every one of us.

ANNE GIARDINI, OC, QC, 2018

at the top of Burnaby Mountain. I wonder how growing up here would have changed me, and I wonder what effect the experience of living and learning here will have on the children who call this community home. They have more freedom than do most children in the city. The streets are safer and more inviting. There are fewer cars, and there is more nature. The university next door is part of their playground and so it will be less mysterious for them when their turn comes to attend SFU or elsewhere as undergraduates.

I both admire and envy the people who built this community from concept to habitation. In this narrative, Gordon Harris lays out the genesis of the idea of UniverCity, and he describes the factors that came together to bring it into being. He describes what the stakes were, and what some of the mistakes were. He tells of the struggles to find a common, workable, achievable concept and to bring it to realization. These are the stories of the agencies, people, governments, builders, funders, visionaries and first residents who agreed and disagreed, bickered and built, made and tore up blueprints, packed bags and moved in and transformed this place from vision to home.

AUTHOR PROFILES

GORDON HARRIS, FCIP

An urban planner, development strategist, and real estate market analyst, with three decades of experience in the public and private sectors, Gordon Harris has been President and CEO of SFU Community Trust since 2007, leading the development of UniverCity as an award-winning community.

Leveraging experience in community planning, and institutional and retail real estate development, Gordon has spent 30 years as an independent consultant, providing urban land planning services, development strategy advice, market intelligence, and economic analysis to public- and private-sector clients in Canada, Asia, the Middle East, Eastern Europe, and Central America.

A popular lecturer on sustainable development, economic development, and planning for an aging population, Gordon was elected to the College of Fellows of the Canadian Institute of Planners in 2009 and to the College of Fellows of the Royal Canadian Geographical Society in 2016. In 2013, he received the Queen Elizabeth II Diamond Jubilee Medal for his contributions to community building in Canada.

RICHARD LITTLEMORE

Richard Littlemore is an author, speechwriter, journalist and consultant who specializes in sustainable development, environmental and social issues, and academic affairs.

Littlemore began his career as a reporter, editorial writer and editor at some of Canada's most influential newspapers (including the Ottawa Citizen and the Vancouver Sun). In 1995, he turned to freelance journalism as an award-winning magazine writer, and to consulting and speechwriting for some of British Columbia's top business and academic leaders.

Littlemore has also written, co-authored or ghostwritten books on everything from real estate development and diamond mining to public relations and environmental activism.

UniverCity on Burnaby Mountain.

Early rendering of UniverCity
on Burnaby Mountain.
Paul Nowarre, 2003.

INTRODUCTION:
BUILDING COMMUNITY

Defining, Designing, Developing UniverCity

Somehow, it looks like it's been here all along.

UniverCity, conceived in the mid-1990s as "a complete, sustainable community" on lands owned by and adjacent to Simon Fraser University's Burnaby Mountain campus, already deserves the description. The High Street is humming, the elementary school is expanding, and just down the street, you can hear the laughter of children at the greenest childcare centre on the planet. UniverCity residents — there are more than 5,000 now — overlap and interact with the students, staff and faculty at Simon Fraser University (SFU). They come together in the town square. They shop for groceries, stop for coffee or meals — book a haircut or buy a bottle of wine at one of the many new businesses that have emerged in the last decade.

UniverCity's physical community connects seamlessly to the iconic SFU campus that Arthur Erickson and Geoffrey Massey designed in the early 1960s. Rising to the east, the new community alternatively hugs and accentuates the mountain contours, cresting the peak and flowing down the gentle slopes. Beyond the civic and commercial centre, the residential development began with a relatively uniform cluster of energy-efficient, mid-rise condominium buildings. But given the passage of time and a change in demand, there is now a greater variety of residential choice — everything from a 17-storey residential tower nearest the commercial centre to a new lower-density neighbourhood, featuring larger, ground-oriented homes for growing families. One of the next residential innovations will be low-carbon-emission rental housing — another in a series of UniverCity projects designed to demonstrate the practicality of some of the most ambitious environmental building standards in the country.

The community's award-winning infrastructure is at once invisible and yet readily apparent. You are obviously not meant to see the new 35-centimetre water line that now protects campus and community alike from interruption to the water supply on Burnaby Mountain. Neither can you see the smaller water lines that radiate out from the District Energy Utility, providing highly efficient heat and hot-water service to all new buildings. The central energy plant will soon be fuelled from locally sourced construction wood waste that would otherwise have gone to the region's landfill. You can, however, see the principal features of UniverCity's innovative stormwater management system. Where other communities have big storm grates draining into industrial sewers, UniverCity has bioswales, infiltration galleries, rain gardens and detention ponds, all of which work together to collect, clean and slowly discharge the nearly two metres of rain that falls on the community each year — all while maintaining the health and vitality of the Stoney Creek watershed, and the salmon-bearing streams and rivers that flow through it.

The mountain rainforest is gloriously in evidence. In addition to community parks and walkways featuring fir trees many generations older than the oldest building, the whole community — along with the university — is surrounded by the Burnaby Mountain Conservation Area, including 576 hectares of forest that is protected in perpetuity.

Of course, that same forest serves to buffer and separate the SFU campus and its vibrant new community from the rest of Metro Vancouver. That was part of the inspiration for building UniverCity in the first place — to complement an otherwise isolated university with a highly functional community that would enrich campus life and, at the same time, serve as an international model for environmentally conscious planning and practice. It was fortunate that the mountaintop already featured the second busiest transit hub in the whole Metro Vancouver region; there were buses bringing SFU students, staff and faculty back and forth from every part of the region — crowded morning and evening, but virtually empty at those times on the reverse journey. That underutilized return service created potential for a new population of counter-directional commuters. SFU Community Trust, UniverCity's development authority, has worked hard to encourage residents to make the best use of that system — to startling success: today, Burnaby Mountain residents commute via transit at three times the rate of those in the region overall. But even that high usage could soon be improved — with an investment that will pay environmental and economic dividends for the mountain and the region. The Metro Vancouver transportation authority, TransLink, is in the advanced stages of planning an aerial transit link — an all-electric gondola. The Burnaby Mountain Link will whisk passengers to the mountaintop from the nearest SkyTrain station at Production Way in less than half the time it currently takes to make the trip in a diesel bus. Two independent reviews, one conducted in 2011 and another in 2017, established that, compared to the existing bus service, the highly efficient gondola system would save enough in operating costs to pay for itself one-and-a-half times over in 25 years. It also would free up so many buses and drivers that the regional transit authority could redirect 57,000 hours of service to other high-demand areas in the region.

So, UniverCity is not so much isolated as secluded. SFU prides itself as the most community-engaged university in the country;

UniverCity is the vibrant new community with which it is most immediately engaged — with greater Vancouver, one of the world's most liveable metropolitan regions, conveniently at its doorstep.

It is, though, the full sense of community that is so impressive at this early stage in the life of this development, says Larry Beasley, a former co-Director of Planning at the City of Vancouver and a busy world expert on modern urban development. Beasley says that the essence of what we understand as "community" usually emerges slowly: "Cities often take a couple of hundred years until they reach some kind of a tipping point when they become a community. No city when it's first designed and built is yet birthed." And yet, Beasley says, UniverCity stands as an exception. In not much more than a decade, it has reached a moment of maturity that is enviable. He says, "UniverCity is not yet recognized on the short list of great sustainable communities — Hammarby Sjöstad or Malmö, in Sweden, inner-city Portland (Oregon) or False Creek (Olympic Village) in Vancouver. But it should be."

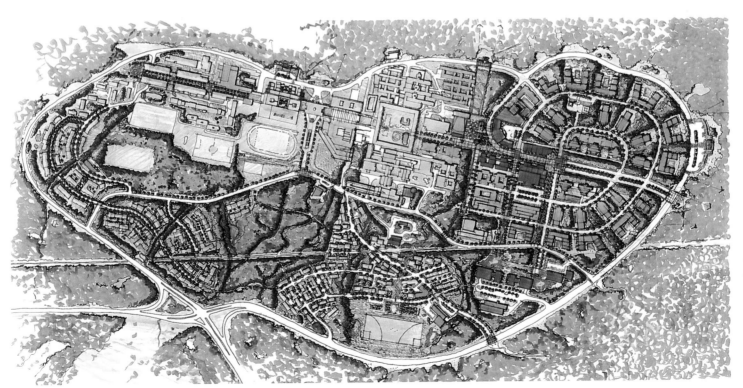

Burnaby Community Concept Plan. Hotson Bakker Architects' Team, February 2000

Simon Fraser University with future UniverCity
site at the top of the image, 2003.

BUILDING COMMUNITY: *Defining, Designing, Developing UniverCity*

As President and CEO of SFU Community Trust since 2007, I can attest to the stature that UniverCity has earned on the international list of model communities. Since 2005, UniverCity has won 30 major awards — locally, nationally and internationally — for high achievement in virtually every aspect of planning and sustainable practice. SFU asked us in 1995 to build "a model sustainable community" and UniverCity is meeting that challenge. Considerable credit for that performance is owed to the Trust's first full-time CEO, Michael Geller. A self-described "accidental environmentalist," Michael's vision and powers of persuasion were crucial in bringing the project through its initial planning approvals and cementing the early partnerships with SFU, the City of Burnaby, and the community's pioneer developers and builders. You also will see, in the following pages, that this kind of success also demands the passion and collaboration of a much larger team. In any enormously ambitious project, there are pitfalls and obstacles waiting for the unwary. Importantly, however, there are lessons to be learned and shared.

> ## "Cities often take a couple of hundred years until they reach some kind of a tipping point when they become a community. No city when it's first designed and built is yet birthed."
>
> **LARRY BEASLEY,**
> **FORMER CO-DIRECTOR OF PLANNING,**
> **THE CITY OF VANCOUVER**

That is one of the dual purposes of this book. The first is to document our story, as a matter of internal review, and for the benefit of those who would join us on the journey to a more sustainable world. Having established a community that others see as fully formed, even if not yet fully realized, we felt the time was right for a thorough evaluation. UniverCity is now home to just over 5,000 residents, on the way to an expected final total between 9,000 and 10,000. In getting to this point, we have laid the foundation of one of the world's most sustainable communities. We also have made some mistakes and have suffered setbacks and indignities, the details of which we are happy to share in the hope that our experience might help clear the path for others. All of this learning will inform our own Board of Directors' strategic plan, keeping us on track as we work toward completing our project.

The second purpose of the book is simply to celebrate. It has been clear from the outset that UniverCity should be more than just an excellent real estate development. We had an opportunity — and a responsibility — to do something spectacular.

We began with one of the most remarkable sites in the world. We have benefited from leaders who were ambitious, capable and inspiring. We've enjoyed support from the best comprehensive university in Canada, and from a municipality, the City of Burnaby, that recognized we were trying to do something special. It's been a challenging experiment, but an unquestioned success.

So, as we accelerate toward completion, this has been our opportunity to take stock of the past, to critique the present and to do all that we can to smooth the path to an even-more fabulous future. With gratitude, optimism and a renewed determination to bring our community to its fullest potential, this, then, is the story of UniverCity.

I thank you for sharing the journey and I hope you enjoy it.

GORDON HARRIS,
PRESIDENT & CEO,
SFU COMMUNITY TRUST

UniverCity on Burnaby Mountain and Simon Fraser University, 2017.

BUILDING COMMUNITY: *Defining, Designing, Developing UniverCity*

Sidebars

Distributed throughout this book are inset pages exploring key insights, lessons, and takeaways that have shaped UniverCity.

These insights apply independently and in combination to inform and inspire the navigation of bold master planning and thoughtful community development.

TOP: **David Gillanders, Gordon Harris, Basil Luksun, Derek Corrigan on hand to receive the American Planning Association's National Planning Excellence Award for Innovation in Green Community Planning, 2008.**

MIDDLE: **Dale Mikkelsen leading an Urban Land Institute Spring Walking tour of UniverCity, 2017.**

BOTTOM LEFT: **A lesson learned.**

BOTTOM RIGHT: **Pat Frouws with future student at the UniverCity Childcare Centre groundbreaking ceremony, 2012.**

BUILDING COMMUNITY: *Defining, Designing, Developing UniverCity*

Parking lots and forest that would become UniverCity, 2000.

1: INCEPTION

A Dream On The Page

19

You begin with a setting of "unsurpassed grandeur."

That was the assessment of Gordon Shrum, the first Chancellor of Simon Fraser University and the man credited with building the institution from scratch in just 30 months. Shrum, a former Dean of Graduate Studies at the University of British Columbia, was serving as Chair of BC Hydro in April 1963 when then-Premier W.A.C. Bennett phoned with a challenge: Bennett wanted a brand new, fully functioning university up and running in time for the 1965 academic year (giving his Social Credit Party ample opportunity to accept accolades before its next campaign for re-election). Shrum, already famous as a man who accommodated neither doubt nor obstruction on the path to a worthy goal, committed before he put down the phone, and Bennett gave him a free hand. As Hugh Johnston writes in the SFU history, *Radical Campus*, "For his first six months as chancellor, Shrum had no one else to answer to: no board of governors, no community group, no advisory committee and no staff. During this half year, he made a series of absolutely critical decisions that set the direction SFU would take."

Not least among these tasks, Shrum chose the location — a pristine mountaintop that was geographically central, even if it was, at the time, rather inaccessible. Shrum wasn't stuck for choices; regional municipalities were falling over one another in the competition to offer land for the new university. The communities of Langley, Delta, Surrey and Coquitlam all offered anywhere between 160 and 320 hectares. Burnaby's first offer, on the other hand, was just 80 hectares, but Shrum loved the location, for a couple of reasons. First, at least by measuring with a ruler on a flat map, it was the spot that the most Metro Vancouver residents could drive to in

30 minutes, the new goal in the burgeoning automobile era of the early 1960s. Second, as Shrum told the selection committee at the time, the view of Burnaby Mountain from his downtown office at BC Hydro was sublime. He said, "I could run both places from here." Through subsequent negotiations, he convinced Burnaby to increase its offering dramatically. He even got the provincial government to throw in a small additional parcel. Thus, SFU began with an endowment of 467 hectares. Access from the then-new Trans-Canada Highway was solved with a new road — six kilometres at a seven percent grade, and little inconvenience at a time when the BC Highways Minister Phil Gaglardi controlled nearly a quarter of the provincial government budget.

The campus was cast in concrete in an image conceived by the brilliant young BC architect Arthur Erickson and his remarkable partner, Geoff Massey. They designed a low-rise and cohesive form, anchored by a stark, classical Academic Quadrangle, all nestled into a saddle along the spine of the mountain. The low profile respected the dominance of the mountain and satisfied strong local preferences. While Gordon Shrum liked the idea of seeing the university from his office in downtown Vancouver, municipal leaders in Burnaby had a different perspective. As reported by SFU's current Vice President, External Relations Joanne Curry in her doctoral thesis on university/community engagement, a Burnaby council member of the day said, "I'm warning you, I don't want to see towers from my office window .... The top of that mountain has got to be trees." The resulting campus — built in just two years and widely celebrated thereafter — was described by another architect, Richard Archambault, as an urban campus in a rural setting. Quoting Hugh Johnston again from *Radical Campus*, it was "a self-contained environment of hard surfaces and formal spaces," surrounded by forest and, to the west, a gentle meadow — which was quickly covered in gravel, and then blacktop, to accommodate the hundreds, and ultimately thousands, of cars that became necessary to serve the commuter campus. Still, for the people of Burnaby, the campus was out of sight, if not always out of mind, a classical academic cloister, comfortably out of the way.

But the concept of the ivory tower — a place of quiet seclusion where students and faculty pursue a life of the mind undisturbed by the distractions of the day-to-day — was never a good fit for Burnaby Mountain. As early as 1972, Dr. Pauline Jewett, then president of SFU (and the first female president of any major

Future site of Simon Fraser University and UniverCity on Burnaby Mountain, 1963.

INCEPTION: *A Dream on the Page*

> **"Part of the problem of the new university is simply the nature of land ownership where the large parcel of land controlled by the university for future expansion creates a no-man's land between the university and the community it serves."**
> **PAULINE JEWETT, SFU PRESIDENT, 1972**

university in Canada), was already lobbying for a change. In an application for funding from a federal Urban Demonstration Program, Jewett said of SFU, "It suffers greatly from its isolation on Burnaby Mountain, both from contact with the community at large and to the deprivation of the students both studying and living there."

The problem may rest in the mythology of the ivory tower. According to Larry Waddell, who today is SFU's Chief Facilities Officer, there is a popular notion that universities were established in out-of-the-way places intentionally and that their isolation was calculated to provide a sense of retreat. But, Waddell says, the practical reality is that, "governments gave universities land on the fringe because that's where the land was available."

By way of illustration, the University of British Columbia was dispatched in the 1920s to Point Grey — then well removed from the city on the westernmost reaches of Vancouver and, even today, still out of the way. SFU went to a mountaintop, not unlike the hillside locations of the University of Northern British Columbia, outside Prince George; Thompson Rivers University, at the edge of Kamloops; and UBC Okanagan, on the far fringe of Kelowna. As Waddell speculates, the ivory tower characterization may have arisen to justify a circumstance that had arisen by accident. "Afterward, perhaps, came the rationale for why universities wanted to be separate. The idea of the cloistered entity, physically designed (as SFU certainly was) to look inward, to get people away from the issues of urban life, to a place where they could think and conduct research."

That said, students and their institutions have long recognized the benefits of being immersed in community. Oxford and Cambridge are obvious models of vibrant university towns with rich cultural and intellectual traditions. A good Canadian example might be Queen's University in Kingston, Ontario. Canada has several big urban campuses such as McGill University in Montreal, the University of Toronto and the University of Alberta in Edmonton, all of which are integrated as social, cultural and economic drivers in the centres of their respective cities. Of course, even McGill was distant and isolated when it was established on the outskirts of downtown Montreal in 1821. "That's another pattern," says consultant and the former co-Director of Planning in the City of Vancouver, Larry Beasley. "If you have time, you just get a big site, grow, and let the world grow around you." But, to quote again from President Jewett's report, "The challenge of the instant university, or all new universities today, is how to introduce this ingredient when the institution is either too removed from the town, or when the town and the institution are too new for this response to have developed. Part of the problem of the new university is simply the nature of land ownership where the large parcel of land controlled by the university for future expansion creates a no-man's land between the university and the community it serves."

Jewett proposed a solution (the specificity of which suggests that the university had already invested a fair amount of energy in developing a plan). President Jewett sought support for the development of "a village community of about 7,120" on land immediately west of the existing campus. "The pervading motive of the plan would be to achieve the density, the scale, the variety and interest of a village: the kind of urban village that complements a university such as Harvard, or Cambridge in England." She even proposed a mechanism, "a system of leasing university land and space to private entrepreneurs" who could then be induced to build residential and commercial buildings and to provide this range of services.

22

There followed complete radio silence. No federal funding was forthcoming and, according to SFU VP Curry's research, the conversation between the university and the City of Burnaby deteriorated into brooding and mutual mistrust. SFU was eager to keep the city out of university business and constantly challenged municipal authority to rule over development decisions. The City responded with concern that the growing university would spill beyond an established ring road, encroaching on a forested area that many people had come to think of as an extension of the adjacent Burnaby Mountain Conservation Area.

The next mountaintop community plan was considerably more sprawling and ambitious. In 1981, in the midst of the hottest real estate market that Canada's West Coast capital had yet seen, SFU engaged the real estate consultant Herb Auerbach to develop a master plan. Auerbach went straight out and hired Arthur Erickson to envision this expansion to Erickson's original creation. The two men read and travelled widely in search of ideas. They looked, for example, at the University of Washington in Seattle and Stanford in Palo Alto. But they found their best inspiration in the hilltop town of Urbino, on the northeast coast of Italy. A World Heritage Site and home to the University of Urbino, the old town is surrounded by a wall that corresponds in its dimensions almost perfectly with the ring road embracing the central SFU campus.

In a voluminous and finely detailed master plan that they presented in April 1982, Auerbach and Erickson laid out a $400-million project with a broad range of objectives, prominent among which was "eliminating the monastic quality of the university ..."

The overarching goal was stated as follows: "It is believed that the creation of an extended community of a certain critical mass, adjacent to and integrated with the University, would become the vehicle through which the University could attain its prime objective, that is: improving the quality of education and research."

Similar to the Jewett plan in the 1970s, this proposal would make room for a village population of just over 7,000, much of it centred around a covered "Main Street" and a Village Square, "a visual and conceptual extension of the existing complex." There would be 2,000 student units in apartments clustered around the square and an adjacent seminar centre, as well as 360 one- and two-bedroom co-op or non-profit housing units. In addition, there would be 1,800

Town of Urbino, Italy

two- and three-bedroom townhouses, 900 units southwest of the main campus and 900 directly to the east. The whole development was designed to be relatively dense by urban standards at 30 to 40 units per acre, but limited to four storeys in height, with no building rising above any existing academic structure.

A defining feature of the new plan was its pedestrian orientation and its innovation. Looking at the challenges faced by cars and buses climbing the mountain sometimes in rain, fog, snow and ice, and at the inevitable expense and damage that would come if the automobile remained the principal means of access, Auerbach, Erickson and the transportation planners at Zolton Kuun Associates proposed construction of a funicular, a cable railway that would

23

LOCATION, LOCATION

There are two takes on location:

In one, you begin with a worthy project and search for the best place to implement it, weighing factors ranging from convenience and accessibility to availability and, always, affordability.

In the other, you begin with a location that you already have and then search for the optimal purpose. What's needed in the neighbourhood? Who are your potential audience and competitors? How might circumstances change even as you are developing your project?

The founders of Simon Fraser University were in the first camp. They had a great project — a brand new university! — so they went looking for the perfect, and optimally convenient, location. And they found it, right in the middle of the region (though, others might later question its isolation on a mountaintop).

As developers of UniverCity, however, SFU Community Trust was in the second camp. We had the location already, and we were challenged to make it all that it could be — and to enhance the liveability and functionality of the university at the same time. We had to figure out what would work — and what mix of homes and services would make it work.

Of course, the other complication about location is that the choices you make have a degree of permanence. You have to remember, moving is expensive. And, despite the romantic mythology, when the earth moves, it's usually a bad thing.

24

UniverCity with Simon Fraser University in the background, 2010

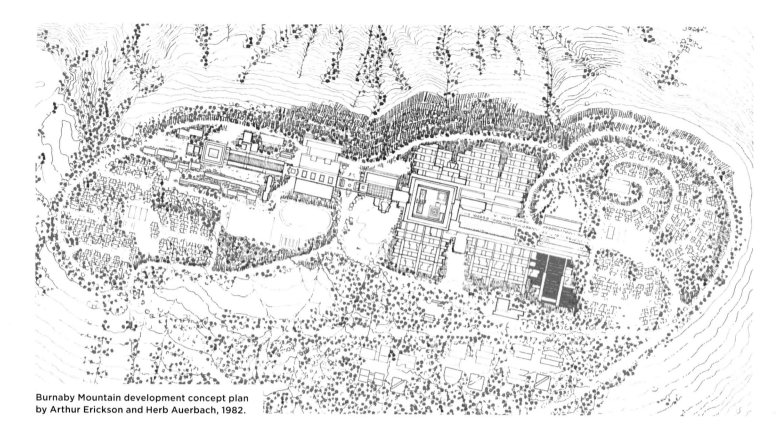

Burnaby Mountain development concept plan by Arthur Erickson and Herb Auerbach, 1982.

travel up the mountain from a large parking lot on Barnet Highway. The math made perfect sense. While the costs for road improvements and mountaintop parking could be expected to reach $25 million in the ensuing 15 years, total expenditures for a $6.5-million funicular and reduced road and parking development would be just $14.75 million. Even better, the planners envisioned a transit link to a high-speed train running from Port Moody to downtown (over the route covered today by the West Coast Express).

It's not clear which one or more of many possible obstacles bumped this plan off the rails. Certainly, the timing was unfortunate. As Auerbach wrote in the master plan, after 18 months of "almost unprecedented house sales volume and price increases, the market has plunged into a severe recession." There was little investment and little optimism for a sweeping new development in an out-of-the-way place. Erickson's ambitious plan was also a costly one: Metro Vancouver house prices in 1981 ranged from $120,000 to $220,000 and condominiums were selling between $70,000 and $134,000. The two- and three-bedroom townhouses in this development were

Neighbours 1982

The Auerbach/Erickson master planning document includes a marketing plan that offers this caution about trying to sell new real estate in a location well known at the time as the Lower Mainland's "radical campus."

"There is some notion, which requires dispelling, that one wouldn't want to live at a university. In the minds of some, Simon Fraser University is a hotbed of dope smoking, sexually liberated and politically radical students, hardly a place to raise a family, or run a shop. Some work will be required to re-establish Simon Fraser University's reputation in the marketplace, and drive home the point of the changing nature of the University."

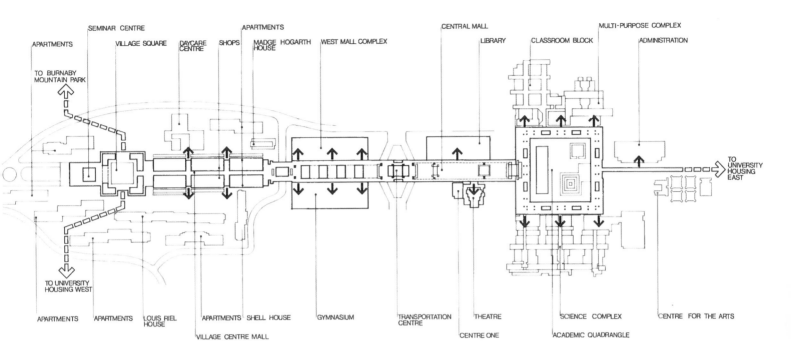

Diagram of Pedestrian Circulation
by Arthur Erickson and Herb Auerbach, 1982.

Labels in diagram:

APARTMENTS — SEMINAR CENTRE — VILLAGE SQUARE — DAYCARE CENTRE — SHOPS — APARTMENTS — MADGE HOGARTH HOUSE — WEST MALL COMPLEX — CENTRAL MALL — LIBRARY — CLASSROOM BLOCK — MULTI-PURPOSE COMPLEX — ADMINISTRATION

TO BURNABY MOUNTAIN PARK

TO UNIVERSITY HOUSING EAST

TO UNIVERSITY HOUSING WEST

APARTMENTS — APARTMENTS — LOUIS RIEL HOUSE — APARTMENTS — SHELL HOUSE — GYMNASIUM — TRANSPORTATION CENTRE — THEATRE — SCIENCE COMPLEX — CENTRE FOR THE ARTS

VILLAGE CENTRE MALL — CENTRE ONE — ACADEMIC QUADRANGLE

expected to be priced between $120,000 and $180,000, a premium price, given the location and the likelihood that services would have developed only slowly. Finally, relations with the City of Burnaby were still chilly. The City only wanted to talk about non-profit housing on the mountain. There was no room for a deal.

Another decade would pass before the pressure for a mountaintop solution began to build again, and this time, on two fronts. First, the provincial government of the day appeared increasingly sympathetic to Burnaby's insistence that the endowment land be returned and protected as park. In 1989, the province had taken 760 hectares from the University of British Columbia's 1,200-hectare endowment on Vancouver's Point Grey to establish Pacific Spirit Park. It seemed likely that SFU's turn was coming. Second, governments in BC and across the country had started to implement campaigns of spending restraint, squeezing or reducing the level of university funding. The theory of an endowment is that it can be used to generate income to support the university's mission of teaching and research. As budgets

tightened, and the university looked like it was facing an increased risk of losing some or all of the endowed land, the theoretical possibility of converting a land endowment into a cash endowment started looking more like an imperative.

But the real turn came in 1993, with the installation of new SFU President John Stubbs. Previously, Stubbs had been president at Trent University in Peterborough, Ontario, where he had successfully developed some of Trent's endowment land. In the process, he had formed a warm relationship with the Peterborough council. When Stubbs moved west, Peterborough Mayor Jack Doris offered to provide an introduction to Burnaby Mayor Bill Copeland. This introduction was a first step toward improving the relationship between the City of Burnaby and SFU.

Stubbs, who moved into the President's Residence, an isolated house east of the main campus, also got a quick and very personal sense of the university's mountaintop isolation. Stubbs says, "There was nothing — and nothing for the students. My wife and I would go

Looking down towards Burnaby and New Westminster, 2013.

"MAKE NO LITTLE PLANS"

This advice comes from Daniel Burnham, the 19th century American architect and urban designer. Burnham said:

"Make no little plans; they have no magic to stir men's blood and probably will themselves not be realized. Make big plans; aim high in hope and work, remembering that a noble, logical diagram once recorded will not die, but long after we are gone be a living thing, asserting itself with ever-growing insistency. Remember that our sons and our grandsons are going to do things that would stagger us. Let your watchword be order and your beacon beauty."

It's worth listening to Burnham — and for more than the poetry of his delivery. Big, ambitious plans telegraph a clarity of purpose and, for that reason, they often build trust; no one doubts your motives. And, of course, a commitment to order and beauty also helps.

Big, clear plans can also make it easier to set small, clear checkpoints. And a great vision deserves a careful, measurable and well monitored process.

29

for a walk in the evening and there wouldn't be anyone there. In the daytime, there would be 18,000 people, but in the evening, they were all gone. The sense of community just withered."

There was yet another reason for the gathering sense of urgency. By the early 1990s, students were becoming more mobile and more discriminating, and, while SFU had emerged as an important research institution often honoured as the best comprehensive university in the country, Stubbs knew that the institution's future depended on being able to offer a rich experience to students, as well as a high quality of life for faculty and staff. Something had to be done to address what Auerbach had called SFU's "monastic" status.

So, SFU was motivated, and the City of Burnaby was at least open to discussion. Stubbs had a set of priorities that fit well with Burnaby's. First, he says, he agreed with the City's ambition to protect the land outside the ring road: "It's such an amazing site, we wanted to build something as environmentally sensitive as possible." Second, Stubbs says he wanted to build a community that would complement the mission and function of the university and enrich the daily lives of those who worked or studied there. Only as a third priority does

"It's such an amazing site, we wanted to build something as environmentally sensitive as possible."
JOHN STUBBS, SFU PRESIDENT

Stubbs talk about transforming the university's physical endowment into cash for the university's operation. The goal was certainly in his mind, he says, but "it was more in the way of securing a longer-term revenue stream."

Negotiations began in 1994, led on the university's side by SFU's then-Vice President External Jack Blaney ("He was the key to all of this. He was the spark plug," Stubbs says), by Blaney's right-hand-man Warren Gill, Vice President, University Relations, and, in Burnaby, by councillors Doug Drummond and Lee Rankin. In 1995, all parties agreed that, in return for Burnaby's support of the development of a community on 65 hectares immediately adjacent to the campus, SFU would return all of the land below the ring road — comprising 320 of the original endowment of 467 hectares. This can be seen as an act of magnanimity, pragmatism, or both.

On the side of generosity, the university was responding to the City's ambition to protect and preserve a popular recreation area and an important green zone near the geographic centre of Metro Vancouver. The transfer made it possible to more than double the size of the Burnaby Mountain Conservation Area, to 576 hectares. On the pragmatic side, the university secured what amounted to a density transfer from the larger property onto the small, accessible parcel immediately next to the campus. Environmentally, that made it possible to maximize the development opportunity (the agreement with Burnaby was for 4,536 housing units) while minimizing the development footprint. Economically, it would also be less expensive to develop and service many units on a smaller piece of property. As a further point of pragmatism, Stubbs says, "It was pretty much impossible to imagine development on a lot of the property [that the university surrendered]; it's all cliffs."

To facilitate the deal further — to get development started, for the benefit of the citizens of Burnaby as well as the university – the City also agreed to transfer a small piece of property at the foot of the mountain, where Burnaby Mountain Parkway turns into Hastings Street. The land was flat, conveniently located next to an existing residential neighbourhood and ready to be subdivided and sold as city lots. The university did just that, generating a profit of more than $10 million — a nest egg that helped fund the expensive process of preparing and servicing land on top of the mountain. Perhaps unfortunately, the transfer also gave rise to a narrative that Burnaby "paid" $10 million to buy back land that it had earlier gifted to the university, (notwithstanding that the provincial government paid Burnaby $5 million to help cover those costs). Even today, Burnaby Mayor Derek Corrigan, who was sitting as a councillor during the early negotiations, says, "Having given SFU the mountain for $1, buying it back for $10 million made a number of us choke. But we knew the opportunity might only come up once, and we knew that, despite the best efforts of the university, they couldn't protect the land as well as we could. So, we swallowed hard and paid the money." And in time, the new, warmer relationship between City and University would prove crucial to keeping the development opportunity on track.

The next step forward in the planning process came with the hiring of Jim Moodie as a project manager to bring together a new master plan. Then-SFU Chancellor Joe Segal chose Moodie as someone with a reputation for keeping the lowest possible profile while doing the highest quality work. Once a planner at the City of Vancouver, Moodie has been working for many years as a consultant and on a few major site developments, including Champlain Heights and the River District. The plan that Moodie's team presented in early 1996 varied dramatically from earlier visions. First, it concentrated development on high ground east of the existing campus, rather than to the west. Second, while it maintained the central development line along the spine of the mountain, it abandoned Erickson's formal structure, choosing to nestle individual lots into the contours of the mountain rather than holding to the strict, straight lines of Erickson's original creation and his later vision.

Perhaps most outrageous, at least from Erickson's point of view, was the proposal to increase building heights to as much as ten storeys. As quoted in David Stouck's authorized biography, *Arthur Erickson: An Architect's Life*, Erickson later condemned this departure from his vision as "a banal, featureless, middle-class neighbourhood ... the unique smothered in the commonplace." Moodie, on the other hand, noted that Erickson's proposed low-rise concrete terraces, stepping down the hill, were both prohibitively expensive to build and challenging to sell, especially to buyers who might already be skeptical about making a large financial investment in a community that was still just a promise on the drawing board. Still, he says, "Arthur and I had been friends. This was a problem."

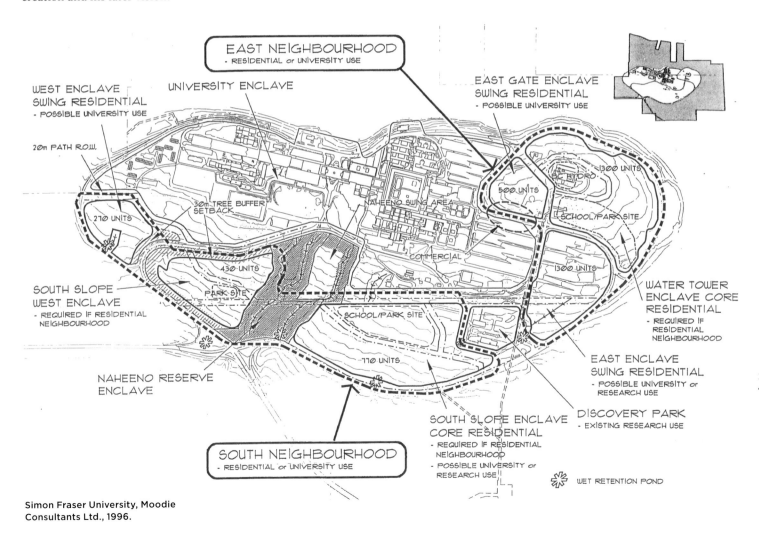

Simon Fraser University, Moodie
Consultants Ltd., 1996.

INCEPTION: *A Dream on the Page*

1996 Burnaby Mountain Community Corporation/ SFU Community Trust

BOARD OF DIRECTORS COMPOSITION

- Four external experts, each having expertise in professions relating to the Trust mandate

- Two members of the SFU Board of Governors

- One student, elected by students

- One faculty member, elected by faculty

- Three SFU Administrators, including the President, Vice President, Finance and Administration, and Vice President, Research

- The Chair of the Community Advisory Committee

- SFU Community Trust President and CEO

- The SFU Director of Facilities Management, *ex officio*

Moodie's plan, however, was otherwise well-received. It honoured the conservationist focus and it was practical to build, even as one group after another intervened to raise the standards of energy efficiency and environmental sustainability. Julie Marzolf, whose firm Marzolf and Associates managed public relations during this period, says that Moodie's willingness to listen to neighbours and public interest groups was essential to the plan's success. They frequently walked the property with everyone from SFU staff and faculty to the stream-keepers who had been working so hard to restore spawning salmon to the creeks coming off the mountain. "Jim's approach is rare," Marzolf says, calling him "the quiet force behind a great many developers."

While much less prescriptive than the earlier Erickson model, the plan mapped well into the City of Burnaby's first Simon Fraser University Official Community Plan, drafted by senior City of Burnaby planner Robert Renger, on the basis of Moodie's work. Even that document lacked much of the detail that the City would have demanded from a private-sector developer, Renger says today. For example, while the City would normally demand very specific descriptions of commercial buildings and public infrastructure, "We basically drew an oval on the map, in the centre of which was the future High Street and town square," and that's just where the high street sits today. There was no subdivision plan and just two residential zonings, one for a low-rise neighbourhood under 4 storeys and one higher-density zoning allowing for buildings up to 10 storeys. Absent greater detail, Renger says, "We tried to lock it [the development] down with some stringent requirements, but we began with a high level of trust."

Burnaby knew that the university planned to lease all development parcels, in part because provincial legislation prohibits universities from selling land. As a result, Renger says, "We knew that they were going to have to live with the consequences of what they did." Unlike a private-sector developer that "finishes a project and walks away, SFU would be involved forever."

The next milestone came in 1998 with the creation of the Burnaby Mountain Community Corporation (BMCC), designated by the SFU Board of Governors to manage development on the university's behalf. The Board clearly stated the BMCC's mandate, starting with:
- To establish a residential community which complements existing and future University development.
- To establish an endowment fund and other sources of revenue to support University purposes.

A third priority didn't quite capture John Stubbs's original call for a development with a light environmental footprint, but it indicated a high level of ambition, calling for "A model community which integrates residential, commercial and academic uses in a manner worthy of local and international acclaim."

The BMCC, which was later renamed SFU Community Trust, had three built-in advantages. First, it could operate legally and practically at arm's length from the university. SFU is the only shareholder, so there is no doubt that, ultimately, the Trust is dedicated to serving the university's interests. But its job is to build a complete, model community that complements the

SFU Community Trust Board of Directors, 2015. From left to right: Howard Nemtin, Japreet Lehal, Patricia Hibbitts, David Gillanders, Gordon Harris, Barry Macdonald, David Poole, Andrew Petter, Julia Kim, Philip Steenkamp, Bev Park, Brian Taylor, Mark Roseland, and Rajiv Kozhikode.

GOVERNANCE MATTERS

In any major project, the complexity of the undertaking should always be balanced by the simplicity of your governance structure.

No such balance would have existed if the oversight of UniverCity had fallen to the SFU Board of Governors, which was already engaged in a highly complex governance task. If students, faculty, alumni, neighbours and interested politicians had all leveraged Board influence to intervene, summarily, in UniverCity development decisions, it would have been a significant distraction from the Governors' main job. So, the SFU Governors created the SFU Community Trust Board with a simple mandate and a single report — back to the SFU Board.

SFU then recruited a remarkable group of subject area experts for the Community Trust Board: developers, real estate lawyers, planners and — importantly — a student, a faculty member and a representative from the neighbourhood. You want this input; you just want it from people who are clearly focused and fully engaged.

The result is that the SFU Community Trust Board has been knowledgeable, disciplined and extremely effective.

university's operation, a goal that might be more difficult if the project was drawn into the day-to-day politics and priorities of every campus lobbyist. Second, the Trust has an independent Board of Directors chosen for a high degree of expertise in planning and development as well as for their responsiveness to the various interests of SFU, its students, staff and faculty, and the neighbours near and far. As a further guarantee of neighbourliness, the Trust also created space for a Community Advisory Committee, comprising students, faculty, staff, alumni and community representatives originally from the Burnaby Mountain Preservation Society and the Stoney Creek Residents Association and later from the UniverCity community.

This concentration on consultation was an absolute necessity, says Jack Blaney, who began this period as Vice President, External Relations but, by the time the Trust came into force, had been appointed SFU President. As you might imagine, given that SFU's official history is entitled *Radical Campus*, "We had a history of students taking over the damn place," Blaney says. "So, we had to be careful. We had to listen. We had to begin with basic values and consult widely. What we learned from the late '60s was that, if you want to get anything done, you have to consult and be open."

The backbone of the Board, and Chair from his installation in 1998 until his retirement in 2016, was David Gillanders, a lawyer with decades of experience in real estate and deep contacts and considerable credibility in the development community. The BMCC (and later SFU Community Trust) began its work under the leadership of two interim presidents, the widely admired and trusted former Dean of Arts, Bob Brown, whose involvement reassured SFU faculty, and another former Director of Facilities Management and later Vice President Administration, Rick Johnson. But as the prospect of actual development drew closer, there was broad agreement that the organization needed an executive officer with experience in real estate development. After careful vetting, Gillanders confirmed the architect, developer and planning consultant Michael Geller as the leading candidate. Geller had worked on major projects around Vancouver, including the Bayshore development in Coal Harbour and the Vancouver Convention Centre, but Gillanders was particularly sold on the public-sector experience that Geller had in managing development on Granville Island when he was with the Canada Mortgage and Housing Corporation.

Participants in the Burnaby Mountain Community Corporation Design Charette, 2000.

It was a controversial choice. Geller's vision — and the direction that he had taken from the university and the Board — clashed directly with the Auerbach/Erickson design, and Erickson became increasingly outspoken in his criticism. As recorded in the Stouck biography, Erickson "denounced the burial of SFU's visionary principles under 'a developer's mercantile blanket'." And he assigned Geller most of the blame, or, as Stouck reported, "Publicly, he denounced Geller as a 'blowhard'", adding that Geller had been hired by another "blowhard", Jack Blaney.

34

Geller is philosophical about the spat. He says now that "Arthur always thought that SFU was a university of the mountain, not a university on the mountain." Having chosen to keep the campus buildings' profile low, Erickson feared that Geller would deface both the site and the stark modernist lines of the original campus with a kitschy collection of Whistler-esque pitched roofs or — perhaps worse — a bland clutch of green-glass high-rises. Erickson also objected to the idea of locating the centre of the new community to the east of the campus on the crown of the mountain; Erickson had envisioned a divided residential community with the village centre to the west, tightly integrated with the university itself, an option that Moodie and company had dismissed as impractical, due to too much overlap between students and residents and too much dispersion of the residential sections. It seemed more like a recipe for conflict than an opportunity to build a village with critical mass.

Although Erickson was hired for a time as an advisor to the university, he ultimately withdrew. Yet, in the result, the power and beauty of his original creation is undiminished by the presence of a

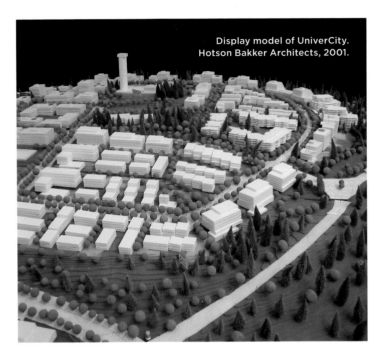

Display model of UniverCity. Hotson Bakker Architects, 2001.

Timing, Timing, Timing

Looking back over 50-plus years in the Metro Vancouver real estate market, it seems clear that UniverCity was a project that arrived at exactly the right moment.

You could identify any number of contributing factors as to why proposals to develop a community on Burnaby Mountain failed in 1972 and 1984. But nothing is as compelling as a graph of housing sales and prices during those periods.

In relative terms, the market was raging when then-SFU President Pauline Jewett commissioned the first serious look at development in 1972. But real estate investors (and government leaders) were becoming increasingly nervous about the effects of inflation and within two years, the bubble burst.

The Erickson/Auerbach plan of the early 1980s was visionary and much more detailed than the Jewett

exploration, but it was also released for public attention at a time when the market had crashed again, and even worse.

Vancouver's hosting of Expo '86 triggered a recovery. As the city's most successful real estate sales professional, Bob Rennie, likes to say, "We invited the world and they accepted the invitation." And they came with gathering enthusiasm during the mid- to late-1990s. As the clock ticked down on Britain's 1997 return of Hong Kong to China, a great wave of immigration and real estate investment created the steepest rise yet in prices and demand. Indeed, there has never been a better time to bring a project to market.

There is, of course, a caveat to the story: the 2008 housing crisis in the United States spilled into Canada, and the Vancouver market took a hit. But it is a credit to the SFU Community Trust Board of Directors that they recognized this as a blip, not a trend, and continued development. Events since have clearly vindicated their good judgment.

supportive community next door. Indeed, the *avant garde* flavour of Erickson's creation remains so strong that, 50 years after being built, his Convocation Mall and Academic Quadrangle remain a favourite location for futuristic backdrops in Vancouver's busy film scene.

By the year 2000, with the administrative and consultative structures in place, Geller organized a four-day charrette, inviting four teams to propose master plans for the property. The winning plan, one that fit elegantly with Robert Renger's first OCP imaginings, was cast by the firm Hotson Bakker Architects (now Dialog). Commenting on that work, architect and urban designer Joyce Drohan says, "Norm Hotson has the greatest skill as a designer. He can read a site and get the best out of it." One of the great challenges, Drohan says, was not just managing the mountaintop terrain, but making the best of it. "That unique flavour of being on top of a mountain is not easy to capture — and they could have chosen to just bulldoze everything and square everything up," she says. "But instead, they knit the development into the mountain, with a strategy of finger-like towers that allow

the woods to integrate and with terrace apartments and a curving perimeter that preserved the panoramic views."

For his part, Hotson says that his team was aiming for a development that was mixed use, with a range of housing types — something that was walkable. They wanted a village and a university that would be integrated without tripping over one another. The key to that integration was to cluster development around a high street and town square where students, staff, faculty and residents could choose to come together, or not. But, Hotson says, the defining characteristic, and one that has come to distinguish UniverCity among some of the most exemplary green communities in the world, was "that the new community should be as sustainable as it could possibly be."

On one hand, this is a return to John Stubbs's desire that any development on the mountain be done in an environmentally sensitive way. But the challenge of developing *sustainably* is a more rigorous test than doing so *sensitively*. Sensitivity is a subjective

Harmony and One University Crescent, two of the early buildings at UniverCity.

Naturalized stormwater infiltration gallery.

GOOD PLANS MUST REFLECT THEIR PLACE

There is no real challenge to driving a square peg into a round hole; you just need a big enough hammer. But once you get it in, it still won't look right.

The modern capacity to engineer almost any terrain is analogous to wielding a big hammer. If you really want straight roads and flat building sites, you can have them, almost anywhere. But you'll spend an extra fortune — and you'll miss the chance to fit something carefully, sensitively — and sensibly — into its environment.

Of course, there will always be debates about what "sensitive" means. When the architects Arthur Erickson and Geoff Massey designed the original SFU campus, they took pride in creating something that hugged the mountain, even as they rendered a stark, formal, concrete spine up the top ridge. And Erickson was famously annoyed when Michael Geller and others advocated later to add taller structures, even though they tucked those new buildings into the mountain contours.

The net result, though, is still a unique community respecting its own topography.

Town Square and Transit Hub at gateway to SFU

Property Development 101: Consultation

It's one of the lessons that people in the development world can never overemphasize: From street planning to tree cutting, the neighbours hate surprises.

This truism, and the corresponding necessity to consult widely and sincerely, was perhaps more urgent on Burnaby Mountain because of the presence of a large population of students and faculty who could be expected to respond with unhelpful enthusiasm if their interests were ignored — or undermined. But the usual approach to community consultation was also complicated by the absence of an actual, proximate community.

So, from the earliest days, the Trust went looking for people with whom to engage. The first Community Advisory Committee included a membership drawn from SFU students, SFU faculty and staff, municipal planning staff and organizations such as BC Housing, CMHC and SmartGrowthBC. But the Trust also sought out people from the nearest established neighbourhoods at the base of Burnaby Mountain, as well as from environmental groups — especially streamkeepers — who had demonstrated an interest in protecting the mountain watershed.

This committee evolved as soon as there was a resident population on the mountain, first to include a Burnaby Mountain Residents' Association, comprising residents (which by this point included members of SFU staff and faculty), business owners and others with an interest in community life, commerce and environmental impact. A new community garden became another crucible for a vocal group of residents who take a keen interest in community affairs and are vocal in defending those interests.

And time and again, the Trust has found that listening to this input early on helps make for decisions that are better, and more easily defensible, as development continues.

INCEPTION: *A Dream on the Page*

UniverCity: Whence Came The Name

Michael Geller, in his new role as president of SFU Community Trust, engaged the Vancouver firm Letterbox Design in the hopes of coming up with a name for the new community. There had been a naming contest, but none of the resulting suggestions had quite measured up to the Trust's criteria or expectations. Geller says that University Highlands wasn't getting enough votes and there was already a Simon Fraser Village. And while some of the other suggestions were tempting, they lacked a direct link to the university, which was crucial.

So, Geller sat down for a Friday afternoon brainstorming session with Letterbox founder, David Hornblow, and then, Geller says, "On Saturday morning, he called me at home and said 'I have it. Can we meet today?'"

Hornblow came in, triumphant, with "a blue *Univer* connected to a green *City*."

Geller says: "I told him it didn't work." But when they rendered the name in one colour and added, 'The community at Simon Fraser,' both men were confident enough to take the idea to the Trust Board Chair and the then-SFU president. Geller concludes: "David Gillanders and (new SFU President) Michael Stevenson liked it and that was what mattered."

Former CEO Michael Geller at the Inaugural UniverCity Community Celebration event, 2005.

> "Sustainable development is development that meets the needs of the present without compromising the ability of future generations to meet their own needs."

THE 1987 BRUNDTLAND WORLD COMMISSION ON ENVIRONMENT AND DEVELOPMENT

measure, but the definition of "sustainable development" is objective and unforgiving. In the words of the 1987 Brundtland World Commission on Environment and Development, "Sustainable development is development that meets the needs of the present without compromising the ability of future generations to meet their own needs." Or, perhaps more simply, it is economic development that is conducted without depleting natural resources.

This idea that UniverCity would be a model not just of good practice but of true sustainability must be credited to Dr. Mark Roseland, the academic and author more than two decades ago of one of the foundational texts in this field: *Towards Sustainable Communities*. Roseland, who teaches at SFU's School of Resource and Environmental Management, realized that his international profile is such that he would have been judged by the UniverCity development whether or not he got involved, so he joined the original BMCC Board as first Chair of the Community Advisory Committee. He was later elected as SFU's faculty representative and his influence has been consistent and consistently positive ever since.

Geller seems only too happy to share the credit on this count. Calling himself "an accidental environmentalist," Geller says his own introduction to sustainable development came when he went to a green development conference in New Orleans early in his tenure as the Trust president and learned about doctors designing for health and engineers designing for safer streets. Geller says now that he was most struck by the reported inverse correlation between density and obesity; that is, that people who live in dense, walkable communities tend to stay fitter and healthier, while those in automobile-oriented suburbs almost inevitably lose the weight-gain battle. Geller says, "I came back and started talking about it."

With Roseland offering validation and encouragement at every turn, the Trust began to implement an increasingly ambitious sustainable policy approach, "I wasn't convinced that doing green roofs would save the world," Geller says. "But I became convinced that if you moved to our development, you would live longer."

One of the first people to test Geller's theory was Michael Stevenson, who took over as SFU President in the year 2000 and immediately asked for a series of meetings with key people involved in the Trust, Geller included. At that point, Stevenson says, "It looked like the project was stalled, but the preliminary planning was very intelligent and it looked like something I would want to embrace. And the university desperately needed to be a place that worked as something other than an office complex for a community of students and faculty."

Stevenson was also highly conscious of the increasing importance of community connection in the life of an effective university. One of SFU's greatest successes to this point had been the establishment in 1989 of a satellite campus in downtown Vancouver. Much was said at the time about this physical outreach as a solution to the problem of making the university's programs more readily available. As it was difficult for the community to come to the university (in its out-of-the-way location), SFU was bringing the university to the community. Stevenson saw the potential development of a community on Burnaby Mountain as a second solution. "It was a chance to bring the community to the mountain," he says. Besides: "No great university exists without also having a great campus environment. You need people and the extra curricular elements that don't come out of the university alone. I was intrigued and made it one of my strategic priorities."

Ultimately, this gave UniverCity the boost it needed to move from a great idea on paper to a promising project in the making.

Measuring Performance: 4 x E = Sustainability

One of SFU Community Trust Board of Directors' early decisions was to endorse a four-part sustainability strategy. The Board began with the three elements that emerged in the 1990s in the so called "triple bottom line" accounting approach, in which progressive businesses were beginning to report not just on their economic performance, but on social and environmental indicators, as well. Given the clear mission of the Trust — to build a community that would complement and support the teaching and research mission of Simon Fraser University, the Board decided to add a fourth leg to the three-legged sustainability stool: education. And with a little editing, they settled on what became the 4 'E's or the UniverCity Four Cornerstones of Sustainability.

ENVIRONMENT:
- Preserve or improve natural resources on Burnaby Mountain.
- Maintain the smallest carbon footprint possible for buildings, transport, and amenities.

ECONOMY:
- Generate revenue to maximize the long-term value of SFU's endowment.
- Encourage innovation in commercial and social enterprises to engage all community stakeholders.

EDUCATION:
- Enhance the education of students and lifelong learners to prepare them for the future economy.
- Energize university life, academic endeavour, and campus activities.

EQUITY:
- Provide a healthy, safe, and affordable place to live and work.

41

42

Nesters Market
in the Hub building.

The BC Liquor store opened in the community in 2016.

Resident playing at Richard Bolton Park.

Turning Communities Of Convenience Into Convenient Communities

One of the biggest challenges in the new century will be un-engineering auto-oriented developments.

Sprawling residential suburbs, business parks, shopping malls stranded in an ocean of pavement: all these seemed like such convenient ideas when everyone aspired to go everywhere in their car. But as energy costs and space constraints mount, it is increasingly evident that, even if you can get there from here, you can't get there on foot.

So, the question becomes: how can you add the services and conveniences of a real pedestrian-oriented community to a development that is isolated amid wide roadways with no sidewalks.

The answer must be to seize every small opportunity and build on (or very near) your successes. As financiers have discovered, modern buyers love transit-oriented developments: they love to live near (or with convenient access to) where they work and play.

So, concentrate features of convenience (such as transit, stores, parks and schools) and people will find you. And when they do, the value of your property will go up — potentially, a lot.

43

FANCIFUL SOLUTIONS MIGHT NOT BE FRIVOLOUS

Here's a prediction: five years after the transit gondola starts running to and from UniverCity — whisking thousands of passengers quickly, quietly and sustainably over daunting mountainous terrain that they never touch — people look back in dismay that anyone ever thought it was a good idea to run diesel buses up and down Burnaby Mountain.

Yet today — in some corners — the very notion of a gondola still elicits patronizing smirks and dismissive comments about treating a university and a small residential community as some kind of mountain resort.

As every good architect and planner knows, the best solutions arise out of the relevant locations. So, if you look at a challenging property and come up with an innovative idea, hold your ground when someone says, "But that's not the way we do things around here."

A funicular, a gondola, a seabus, a bike lane! — transportation options that serve people (and not necessarily people-in-cars) often land lightly. But it doesn't mean they're lightweight.

Schmitten cable car cabins in Zell am see, Austria.

schmitten.at

SCHMITTEN
in Zell am See

INCEPTION: *A Dream on the Page*

Siblings head to classes at University Highlands Elementary School.

BUILDING COMMUNITY: *Defining, Designing, Developing UniverCity*

DEAL-MAKING MATTERS

1. LISTENING IS THE KEY

There's a lesson that every good salesperson or deal-maker must learn: willing parties don't always look willing when the negotiation first begins.

Here's something else: you have to ask the other party what they want, or what they fear. And you have to really listen to the response, because the solution rests in their answer. "Win-win" is only a tired cliché if you have no interest in negotiating a mutually beneficial agreement.

Simon Fraser University went through more than a decade of miscommunication with the City of Burnaby and, after every short, unsatisfactory meeting, people went back to their offices and constructed stories to justify their own positions and to vilify their "ill-informed" opposition. Only when both sides sat down, identified their interests and made an effort to understand the interests and concerns of the other did the impasse disappear.

So, be aware that deal-making involves some work, but it's often easier than it first seems. And good deals work for everyone.

2. CREATIVITY TAKES TWO

If you look back over most negotiations, it's usually easy to identify — and smile about — that early stage deal-breaker, the one detail that looked like it would never be resolved.

On Burnaby Mountain (as in most places), the issue came down to a combination of ambition, power and money. Simon Fraser University wanted to develop its land (inside the ring road), but didn't have the authority or the cash to get started. The City of Burnaby wanted to prevent SFU from developing its land (outside the ring road), had the authority and certainly didn't want to give up any money.

But once the parties realized that their interests resolved at the ring road, there was an opportunity to get creative. Specifically, Burnaby recognized it could achieve its goal of protecting 320 hectares of park by giving up a small piece of land that would have been a political nightmare if the City had tried to develop it directly.

So, don't let your focus on the goal distract from creative solutions.

INCEPTION: *A Dream on the Page*

Initial clearing to make way for UnverCity development, 2003.

BUILDING COMMUNITY: *Defining, Designing, Developing UniverCity*

2: CONSTRUCTION

Shovels In The Ground

People in British Columbia take their trees seriously. Perhaps it's the weather. Maybe the best way to adapt to a place that gets nearly six feet of rain every year is to nurture a deep appreciation for the gifts that rain brings, not least the spectacular temperate rainforest. Before the early West Coast settlers started logging Burnaby Mountain in 1903, its slopes were thick with Western hemlock and with Douglas fir trees that were recorded to be up to 3.5 metres in diameter. But as those towering conifers fell to the saw, a new forest emerged, and by the end of the 20th century, this second-growth was lush and beautiful and full of transitional species like bigleaf maple and red alder, growing decadent and giving way to a new generation of hemlock, fir and western red cedar. So, everyone was aware of the contradiction and the potential for resistance as SFU Community Trust came closer to the day that it would have to start razing the forest to make way for "a model sustainable community."

From some perspectives, logging hardly seemed necessary. Jack Blaney, who was SFU President at the time, says that when he looked east from his office window, "It was blacktop in every direction." The commuter campus had been forced to provide so much parking that, "It looked like we could build a village without cutting down any new trees." But then: if they built a new community on the site of existing lots, the university — or the Trust — would have to clear an equally large patch of property on which to replace the parking. There was no escape.

So, says former Trust Chair David Gillanders, "The first decision (then-Trust President Michael) Geller and I made was to cut down the trees. We agonized for three weeks, but then we decided to cut down all the trees from the first three phases (of anticipated development) at once."

Stormwater Management pond construction, 2013.

CONSTRUCTION: *Shovels in the Ground*

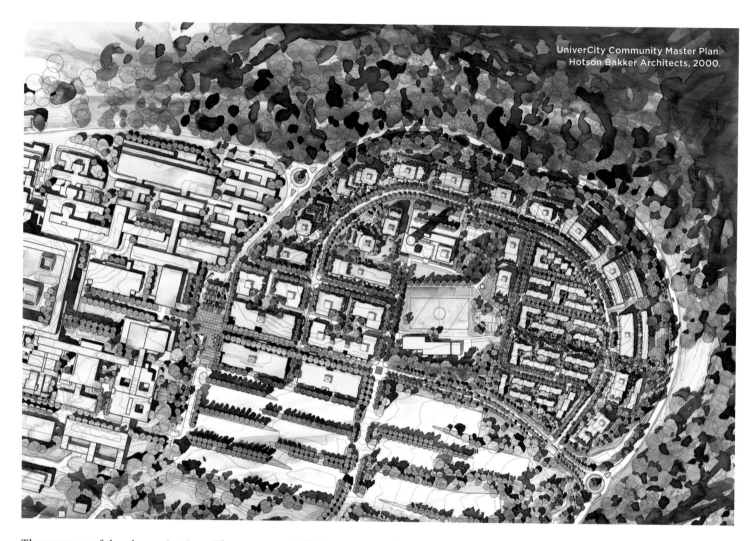

They were careful and conscientious. They announced their intentions publicly and clearly. They retained big trees wherever possible and, following the innovations in the Hotson Bakker master plan, they maintained landscape bulges to preserve what Geller calls the sense of an urban place within a forest. They arranged the logging for the heat of summer, when all the nesting birds would have flown (and, coincidentally, when most of the students and many of the university's faculty and staff were away from the campus). The operation went off without a hitch. Nearly.

It was 2002 and Chris Hartman had just signed on as SFU Community Trust's new Director of Development. Hartman had studied geography as an undergraduate at SFU before going on to

the University of Calgary for a degree in Urban Planning. But he says that, in 2002, he was unsentimental about the environment. "I'm a guy who likes to cut down trees and build roads." It was his clear understanding that that was what the Trust had hired him to do: "to move forward, to get pipe in the ground — to bring life to the development plan."

So, Hartman was disappointed, at 7:30 a.m. on the day that logging had started, to hear that a lone protester had roped himself to the front of a backhoe that was otherwise supposed to be digging out a large, old cedar stump. Hartman responded by doing the only thing he could think of. He set off in the direction of the protester and, on the way, "I bought him a cup of coffee." And not much later, a

52

second cup, the powers of which worked in just the way you might imagine. Seeing the young man in growing discomfort, Hartman said, "Listen, why don't you let me take you to my office and we can have a conversation."

In the years since that first and most-significant pruning, environmental activists, SFU students and faculty have all stood witness to the Trust's commitment to balancing allowable development with the protection of the forest. The design first sketched by Jim Moodie and company and refined by Norm Hotson

Once past the obvious and inevitable first step, clearing land and laying infrastructure in the ground, the Trust faced a strategic question: What do you build first? The answer was both inevitable and impossible: Everything.

made way for "green fingers" of forest that are integrated in the community, providing buffer zones and park-like pockets. The Trust now counts the lack of further protests as a tacit endorsement of that approach.

Once past the obvious and inevitable first step, clearing land and laying infrastructure in the ground, the Trust faced a strategic question: What do you build first? The answer was both inevitable and impossible: Everything.

"It was the classic chicken or egg problem," says Geller. "Do you build commercial? Housing? An elementary school? Well, you need it all — now." This was the starkest reflection of the Trust's level of ambition. UniverCity was not an infill project. It wasn't a matter of adding a student residence here or a service building there. The goal was to build a complete community. In which case, Geller points out, "Nothing is viable until everything (and everyone) is available." You can't attract residents to a "community" until there is a place for them to shop for, at the very least, the necessities they need from day to day. But you can't attract shopkeepers until you have a residential population adequate to support even the smallest of small businesses. It's also hard to attract parents without a childcare centre or a school. There would be little incentive for SFU staff and faculty to buy a home on Burnaby Mountain, to be closer to their work, if the first

thing they had to do every day was pile their kids in the car and drive to some distant childcare or school.

This was one of several times when the Trust was able to do something that a private-sector developer would have been unable or unwilling to do: invest, patiently, for the long-term return. Certainly, other developers invest large sums, and they wait what sometimes seems an eternity for a return. It's the nature of the business. On almost any development, you have to assemble land and work through an expensive and time-consuming process of planning and securing approvals. You have to lay in services and build buildings or sell lots. Only near the end of the process do you begin to recover your original capital, and only at the very end do you find out whether the project has made a profit. Even then, and even if you began with your own stake and so you haven't been paying interest all along on borrowed money, you still must consider your opportunity costs, the interesting and profitable things you might have done with your money had it not been tied up all that time. So, most developers are in a hurry. They are looking at a five-to fifteen-year timeline, and they're impatient to reach the endpoint.

Left to right: City of Burnaby Councillor Colleen Jordan, former SFU President Michael Stevenson, former MLA Harry Bloy, former CEO Michael Geller, and David Crossley, first student member of SFU Community Trust board at the Groundbreaking Ceremony, 2003.

53

Lessons Learned: Stirring The Retail Mix

Looking back at UniverCity's early retail bumps, it would have been smart to set aside a budget — something between $2.5 and $5 million — for supporting new retailers. Even though the Trust set highly favourable rates, they weren't enough. There was a period when the vacancy rate rose to nearly 40 percent, after which we wound up letting several failing retailers out of their leases since there was no point in doing otherwise.

Once again, the priority was to reassure prospective buyers that they would have the services they needed, so setting a reasonable and predictable budget for that purpose would have been wise. And it probably would have been more pleasant to explain to the Trust Board than ongoing losses that amounted to something between $2.5 and $5 million.

The other lesson flies in the face of an early UniverCity preference for "mom and pop" style independent retailers over larger retail chains. The Trust was trying to develop a unique neighbourhood look and feel, so it avoided big-name chains. But experience showed that the moms and pops of the retail world generally don't have the deep pockets necessary to ride out a long, lean period before a new retail location becomes truly profitable. On the contrary, the people with staying power tend to be the well-capitalized, patient retailers with multiple locations and a sophisticated management team.

Another developer might look more closely at the most important goal of providing a reasonable retail mix to residents and work open-mindedly with whoever was going to be most able to deliver the services that residents want and need.

The Trust, on the other hand, was thinking in centuries. It was never going to sell land. Instead it was selling 99-year leases on property that would never completely leave the hands of the university. It made sense, therefore, to build the critical components at the front end, even if there was no prospect of payback in the near term.

So, the Trust began by leasing property for two residential developments: Harmony, and One University Crescent, a 113-unit marquee building that would include a residence for the SFU president to replace the remote house presidents had occupied until then, custom-designed with the assistance of then-president Michael Stevenson. These were both projects of the kind of ambition and quality that would establish UniverCity's reputation as a worthy destination for new home buyers with no previous connections to the mountain, as well as those who already had an association with SFU.

As those two projects were about to get underway, the Trust built The Cornerstone, a mixed-use, commercial/residential building that would anchor University High Street and provide the first shops, restaurants and commercial office space. This was a loss leader, a product for which there was no current demand, and in 2003, little demand anticipated for several years to come. Absent a market population, no commercial tenants could be expected to sign a lease without significant subsidy. As it turned out, even with a subsidy, few of the optimistic early businesses would survive the long wait for customers. The imagined community was still years from reaching critical mass.

Of course, at this stage of development, the very concept of critical mass was still a matter of mystery. There is no planning school reference book that states, categorically, the right population number for a sustainable small community. Lots of sources speak to one element or another. For example, school districts have good calculations for the optimal number of homes in a catchment area (although the number can change radically over time as new communities "mature" and children grow up and move away). And many retailers have detailed guidelines for where to locate stores, according to tallies of surrounding population and proximity to competition.

One University Crescent at UniverCity.

Weekend visitors enjoying a pit stop at Nesters Market after a bike ride up Burnaby Mountain.

Still, trying to find an ideal community size is tricky. You can look to high-functioning small communities — places like Nelson, BC, pop. 10,000 — without really establishing whether that exact size was a decisive factor in the community's success. You can find smaller towns — often associated with small universities — that also work perfectly well; for example, the Nova Scotia homes of Acadia University (Wolfville, pop. 4,300) or St. Francis Xavier University (Antigonish, pop. 4,500). But even if you satisfied yourself that you have an ideal number for a stand-alone community, that population wouldn't necessarily work as well when set within a larger urban area. In regions like Metro Vancouver, community populations frequently overlap and neighbourhoods bleed into one another. Even in cases where there is some geographic separation, it's hard to anticipate when individuals in any particular community might choose to take their business elsewhere, thereby increasing the profitability of a distant set of stores while endangering the viability of those nearby. The automobile makes these calculations yet more challenging. Once people climb into their cars, they can make very different decisions about what they consider convenient. They might drive right past the "handy" commercial street in their own neighbourhood in favour of a 20-minute trip to a shopping centre or big-box store that has free parking, lower prices and a larger selection.

For UniverCity, the choice of an "ideal" target population came out of the 1990s negotiations that gave rise to the first Official Community Plan (OCP): The City of Burnaby fixed the number of allowable dwelling units at 4,536. Whether you interpreted that as an entitlement or a cap, it still set a possible target population at a little more than twice that number. That number had, as it happens, immediate appeal. Both an elementary school and a grocery store require a population of between 8,500 and 10,000, so 4,500 units is about right for reaching that critical mass. As Trust Board Chair David Gillanders says now, "We needed the kind of development to achieve a community population of between 9,500 and 10,000. That was on my radar from day one."

Yet, these factors didn't fully answer the critical mass question. The plans and permissions enshrined in the OCP contemplated four different development sites, all within the university ring road, but scattered around the southern and eastern fringes of the existing SFU campus. If you dispersed 4,500 units among these four sites, you might find that you had built an auto-oriented, residential suburb instead of a coherent community. The cross-campus distances are such that, if you distributed the residences (as Arthur Erickson had once imagined) but concentrated the commercial development in the East Neighbourhood High Street, shoppers from the southern and westernmost properties might not be inclined to jump into their cars for pretty much every trip to the store. Even if the High Street was the destination of original intent, once in the car — well, there's a Costco and more seven minutes down the hill.

It became clear that, just as the community needed everything at once, it also needed everything in one place, a realization that fit well with the Trust's sustainability mandate. The East Neighbourhood is perfectly walkable. Everything within it can be reached on foot in five to eight minutes including the second-busiest transit hub in Metro Vancouver. If the Trust could take advantage of that proximity and make it convenient for residents to move around the community on foot and to choose transit when they commuted off the mountain, less space could be dedicated to roadways and, especially, to parking. Less space dedicated to roads and parking spots would mean shorter walking distances between

It became clear that, just as the community needed everything at once, it also needed everything in one place, a realization that fit well with the Trust's sustainability mandate.

destinations, an advantage that the Trust would realize several times over within the first 10 years of construction.

It's no accident that we have come this far in the discussion of critical mass without using the term "density." On the urban planning battlefield, density has become a highly politicized word, especially among people who are working to "protect" their single-family neighbourhoods from "densification." In Vancouver, a former mayor, Sam Sullivan, coined the term EcoDensity in an apparent effort to point out the environmental benefits of consolidating population on a smaller footprint, to maximize land value and reduce urban sprawl. (It would be wrong to blame this campaign for Sullivan's ensuing drop in popularity, but it would be naïve to think it wasn't a factor.) The other loaded word, almost an epithet among opponents to densification, is "tower." Many people, including an increasing number who will never be able to afford the astronomically expensive single-family homes in Metro Vancouver's most desirable neighbourhoods, recoil at the suggestion that a high-capacity building should be added to a residential neighbourhood.

UniverCity has consistently offered proof-of-concept on the EcoDensity front without ever being part of the politicized debate. It has helped that the original trade-off was so obvious: the Trust traded 320 hectares dedicated in perpetuity to a conservation area in return for development on just 65 hectares (and, ultimately, likely even less). People could see and walk through the benefit of this trade-off right next door. But from the outset, the Trust described its forms of development not as "dense," but as compact and walkable. And it made sure that these descriptions are accurate and never merely promotional spin. For example, the Trust has invested in walkability by preserving pedestrian rights of way and building good walking trails throughout the community, and it has taken care to provide parks and open spaces that contribute to the community's liveability.

"Sales" Challenges:
Out Of The Way, And Out Of The Ordinary

In UniverCity's earliest days, some of Metro Vancouver's most successful real estate developers questioned whether the mountaintop community could ever succeed. They argued that, aside from those directly associated with Simon Fraser University, few people would wager mortgage money on a home that was both out of the way — and, literally, not even for sale.

The concern arose from the geographic isolation that had inspired the plan to build a new community. It's true that founding Chancellor Gordon Shrum chose Burnaby Mountain for SFU's first campus because of the site's relative convenience; it was accessible to the largest number of surrounding communities in a 30-minute drive. But 35 years later, it still didn't feel convenient. Even from the foot of the mountain, your destination is still six kilometres distant and 300 metres straight up. On a bicycle, the fittest 20-year-old will struggle for the better part of 30 minutes to conquer that hill. And while there are two roads leading to the top (Gaglardi Way and Burnaby Mountain Parkway) and while they join in a loop around the peak, they still serve as a metaphorical dead end. You don't happen by UniverCity on your way to somewhere else; you have to make the trip on purpose.

The other potential sales obstacle was that the Trust was looking for buyers who would pay top dollar for properties that were not, in the conventional sense, for sale. SFU's endowment came nominally from the City of Burnaby, but legally from the province of British Columbia. The province gifted that land on the condition that if any time it became surplus to university needs ownership would revert to the Crown. Hanging out a "for sale" sign would be tantamount to surrendering the property.

The University of British Columbia, which had an endowment six times the size of SFU's, pioneered a way to overcome that hurdle. Beginning in the late 1980s, UBC began developing its property and making parcels available by 99-year lease, with the cost of the lease payable up front. Private-sector developers snapped up the land, and built and sold condominiums at prices very near the market rate for comparable, fee-simple properties. But it was far from certain that UBC's success would translate to SFU. UBC is on Point Grey, edging onto some of the most valuable residential land in the country and a 20-minute drive from downtown Vancouver.

There was, therefore, some trepidation at the Trust when it came time to lease the first parcel. Then-Trust President Michael Geller, who had worked previously with many of the region's most prominent developers, did a considerable amount of advance work, reconnecting with industry leaders to make sure they understood the opportunity. At least one of those developers told him he was out of his mind to be proposing high-density residential in such an out-of-the-way location. So, the Trust set up a two-stage process. Any developer who wanted to bid on the property would first have to pre-qualify. Geller says now that it was a safety measure to ensure that the winning bidder was going to be a developer with the resources and reputation to fulfill the Trust's expectations. Bluntly, Geller says, "We were worried about attracting developers who would do high-quality work."

In hindsight, there was no need to fret. When Geller and his staff opened the pre-qualifying bids, there were 24 submissions, 23 of which fulfilled nearly every preliminary condition. "But at the end of the day," Geller says, "there was only one, clean bona fide bid." It came from developer and philanthropist Michael Audain's firm, Polygon Homes, a trusted option that was reassuring for everyone involved. The Trust has gone on to lease 20 more major properties to developers, including Millennium, Intergulf, Liberty, Porte, Mosaic, Vancity, and 8th Avenue. Polygon alone has developed four more buildings. While you might have expected that purchasers looking at a 99-year lease would want a significant discount on the land compared to what they might pay if it was for sale out-right, the circumstance, for SFU Community Trust, has been surprisingly favourable.

Two things appear to have worked in the Trust's favour. The first may reflect the Trust's relationship to SFU. Universities are generally respected as stable, long-lived institutions with the resources to protect the integrity and value of the community over the long term. The market has shown complete confidence in our ability to stand by the University's lease obligations. Second, the price of land in Metro Vancouver continues to rise at rates faster than anywhere else in Canada, and there is fierce competition for developable properties in high-value locations including Burnaby.

The notion of leasing was considered in the 1970s and again in the 1980s, in SFU development proposals that were left on the shelf. In 1982, a major Vancouver real estate analyst estimated that the market would demand a discount of between 20 and 25 percent. Thanks to the factors above, and to the quality of the product, any actual discount on UniverCity leasehold property is now in the low-single digits. Indeed, the Trust consistently receives bids that look very much like "full price" even though ownership will revert to SFU in 99 years. Clearly, purchasers trust the process and trust that Simon Fraser University will continue to protect the values of their investment.

As to building typology, there was significant early opposition to the construction of towers at UniverCity. Part of the resistance arose from the contention of the original SFU architect, Arthur Erickson, that the campus (and any subsequent development) should be limited to four storeys in order to hug the mountain's profile. Further opposition arose from early concern among Burnaby city councillors that the bucolic image of their green mountain might be subsumed by urban spires. But an important part of the resistance to all towers is the antipathy that people feel to the stark, isolated (and often failed) tower developments first promoted in the early 20th century by the Swiss-French architect Le Corbusier. Think of the worst examples of "council housing" in the United Kingdom, or "the projects" of New York City.

The real issue, though, is often not the towers themselves, but the space in between them. There is a world of difference between forested walking trails and wide roads and parking lots. With all that in mind, the Trust ensured that most new parking went underground. And, per the original Official Community Plan, building height was first limited to 33.5 metres or 10 storeys, and the tallest of those short towers were situated low on the mountain's shoulder, where the line of sight flowed naturally into the surrounding forest.

While we have been cautious about using the term "density," we have shown less restraint in talking about "sustainability" — a word that may be less controversial, but should be equally suspect. UniverCity has been described innumerable times as "a model sustainable community." But the literal accuracy of that claim is problematic. An earlier chapter addressed the literal definition of "sustainable development." One of the best definitions of the word "sustainability" appears in the *Oxford English Dictionary*. It is "economic development or the utilization of natural resources [that is] able to be maintained at a particular level without causing damage to the environment or depletion of the resource."

No damage. No depletion. That's a very high standard.

Of course, many people use the word sustainable without ever intending to meet that test. Terry O'Reilly, creator of the great CBC Radio program, *The Age of Persuasion*, has explained why. O'Reilly says that sustainability is what advertisers refer to as a "squishy" term. While he doesn't define "squishy," it's probably this: in the last

COMPACT AND WALKABLE

Language has power and certain words can be explosive. Density, for example, has taken on different meanings for different people. It sounds good to developers, for whom an increase in allowable density can equate to an increase in the value of their land. But single-family residents who hear "density" may imagine the worst aspects of the boisterous inner city — crowded and filled with ne'er-do-wells.

So, if you are making the case for pedestrian-oriented neighbourhoods with sufficient population to support good local services, you should be describing the features that make a community welcoming and successful, not arguing over the controversial cause. For example, most of us respond favourably to the notion of a community that is compact and walkable. We love the notion of a short stroll to a park, a store or a convenient connection to excellent transit.

Leave the planning language to planners. If you want people to like your project, you need to describe the things that people like.

couple of decades, sustainability has been used to mean so many different things that in the minds of the general public it has come to hardly mean anything at all. In a world where a host of high-net-cost consumables are pitched as being green, sustainability has become part of the vast lexicon of greenwash — like "clean coal."

So, an admission: UniverCity is not — yet — a model of sustainability (though we'll talk more later about the progress we are making toward that goal). It has, however, done a great deal that is well worth emulating.

One of the first, sweeping and so far, most-influential initiatives has been to establish, enforce and prove the attainability of ambitious Green Building Guidelines. Long before the goal of full sustainability was even clear, much less realistic, the Trust committed to achieving the highest possible standards in energy, water efficiency, and stormwater management. But in 2002 and 2003, as the Trust was preparing its first parcels for lease, there were no proven standards with which to challenge prospective developers. (LEED®, for Leadership in Energy and Environmental Design, which later became something of an industry standard, was still in a developmental phase.) So, the Trust hired Heather Tremain and Robert Brown of ReSource ReThinking Building to create a set of guidelines, and later engaged Tremain directly to manage the Trust's most successful demonstration projects.

Tremain says today that creating the guidelines was sensitive work in the early part of the 2000s. There were a few examples at that time of industrial or commercial buildings with advanced green building *bona fides*, and Tremain and Brown had worked on a high-profile Vancouver residential project called Ardencraig, "but we were pioneering in that space," she says. To make matters more interesting, the Trust was trying to attract developers to a field that was partly "green" and partly "brown." Some of UniverCity's development area was still forested, but much was already covered and paved for SFU parking (as many as 2,000 spaces would be repurposed). Tremain says, "Many people thought it was already complicated enough."

But the Trust forged ahead, setting targets in 2010 that all new homes be 30 percent more energy efficient and 40 percent more water efficient than was specified in the Model National Energy Code for Buildings. The Trust also offered a 5 percent density bonus if developers could outperform the energy efficiency target by 50 percent, and a further 5 percent bonus if they could demonstrate

Long before the goal of full sustainability was even clear, much less realistic, the Trust committed to achieving the highest possible standards in energy, water efficiency, and stormwater management.

enhanced stormwater management capacities. And from the outset (though not always without complaint), developers submitted bids that committed to meeting the minimum standard and, most often, reaching for the bonus.

Tremain's demonstration project, mentioned above, is the award-winning Verdant, a low-rise residential building that was designed to honour all components of the Trust's Four 'E's — Environment, Economy, Education, and Equity. The overarching goal in this project was to make housing more affordable to people who work at the university, to help SFU attract and retain faculty and staff in one of Canada's most expensive housing markets. To do so, the Trust partnered with Vancity Enterprises, a socially-responsible financial institution that is also the largest credit union in Western Canada. The Trust leased the land for this 60-unit family housing project at 30 percent below market value, and in return Vancity agreed to sell units at 20 percent below market value, and to protect that differential in perpetuity by placing a covenant on title.

Green trails and walking paths within UniverCity.

CONSTRUCTION: *Shovels in the Ground*

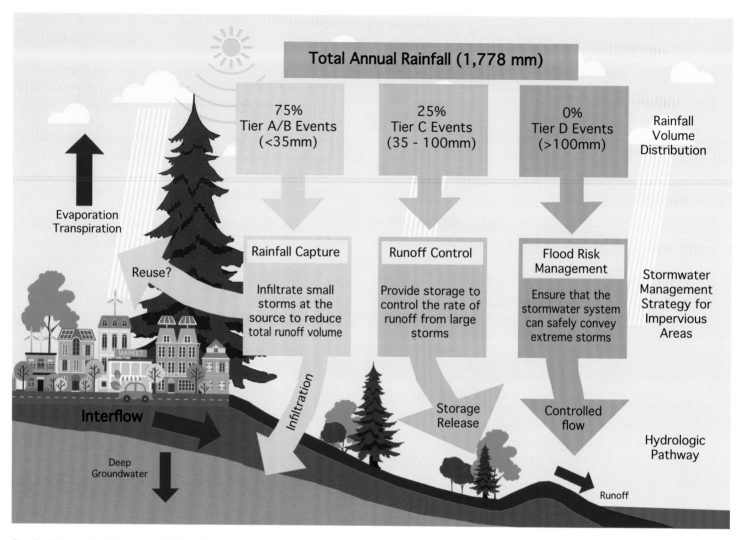

On-site Stormwater Management integrated strategy for managing the complete spectrum of rainfall events.
Burnaby Mountain Watercourse & Stormwater Management Plan, CH2M Hill, 2002.

Everyone involved helped reach this target. For instance, instead of aiming for a normal developer's profit of say, 15 or 20 percent, Vancity agreed to a fixed development fee of 10 percent. It kept marketing costs to a minimum (1.5 percent vs. 3.7 percent), and was able to limit construction to a hard-cost average of $145 per square foot, compared to a typical average at the time of $190 to $200 per square foot. Yet, on completion, this was the most energy efficient wood-frame residential building in Canada. In addition to exceeding requirements under the SFU Community Trust Green Building Guidelines, Verdant was also designed to meet LEED® Gold

certification through energy efficient construction, improved air quality and water conservation measures.

Verdant was able to reach some of its impressive performance standards because Vancity invested in high-efficiency, and higher-cost base infrastructure, including geo-exchange heating and solar hot water. In normal circumstances, these features create what is called a "green premium," the higher purchase cost often associated with innovative and efficient building types. In an expensive market such as Metro Vancouver, this is a premium that developers

Stormwater Management: A "Sewer" System That Even Salmon Can Love

Fir trees are not BC's only iconic species. Consider salmon. Burnaby streamkeepers had spent decades working to restore salmon bearing streams that flow off Burnaby Mountain, including several that drain into the now-healthy Brunette River, so there was some early consternation over the prospect of a whole new community blossoming on top of Burnaby Mountain. New development is generally the worst thing for salmon streams. You have two issues, pollution and flow. On the pollution front, roads and walkways are inevitable sources of oily residue and other material that can be death to salmon and anything else hoping to survive downstream. As to the matter of flow, pavement and rooftops are impermeable, so rainfall quickly becomes stormwater, creating sudden surges that can flood and scour creeks and streams all the way down the mountain. Either that, or developers build storm sewer systems that whisk the water away from the neighbourhood and past any waiting fish, who are left thereafter in a shallower creek. In contrast to that model, a forest floor, thick with fallen leaves, needles, salal, Oregon grape and trailing blackberry is a perfect medium to moderate that flow, filtering out impurities at the same time.

With all that in mind, the Trust set one of its first, clear and measurable environmental performance targets. In the words of Gabor Vasarhelyi, an engineer who helped develop and refine the Trust's award-winning stormwater management system, "We were going to build a high-density development in such a way that salmon, swimming at the bottom of the hill, would think there was still a forest up there." The approach was an adaptive management strategy crafted by the engineering firm CH2M and maintained for most of the first eight years by Vasarhelyi. At the design stage, Vasarhelyi and company would explore best practices in current literature and design out a system with the kind of features they hoped would achieve the goal. These features included permeable pavers, bioswales, green roofs, infiltration galleries and holding ponds. Any one of these features might appear in any good modern development,

but Vasarhelyi and the Trust took an important second step and bound themselves in the process to a much a higher standard. Most developers decide their level of ambition (or measure the demands of regulation) and then design and build their stormwater system accordingly. Then they walk away, leaving municipal authorities to observe the level of success and manage the system without any real option to amend it after the fact. At UniverCity, Vasarhelyi worked with the Trust to monitor and test the performance of the whole system as they developed each new phase, checking to see whether the flow rates and infiltration capacities were adequate. And if, for any reason, they were disappointed, they redesigned the next phase of development, changing or adding features to ensure that the ultimate net flow over the entire project would meet or exceed their original targets.

They were, indeed, disappointed on several occasions along the way. It turns out that most of the mountain-top is sandstone, which was almost perfectly resistant to early attempts to induce infiltration. In the first phase, Vasarhelyi says, "we learned a lot." And in subsequent phases they changed the approach accordingly, adding more infiltration area and more features to moderate flow and ensure that runoff was adequately filtered for impurities. Performance, since, has been more than acceptable. The system has weathered two 100-year storms in a span of three days, proving a capacity that outstrips regulatory requirements and appears to meet the original test: happy salmon. While the salmon have never called to complain or congratulate, the Trust has taken great reassurance from the endorsement of professional watchers, and a host of awards that recognize the integral role that our stormwater management system has played in the success of our overall community plan.

The Stormwater Adaptive Management Plan continues to be closely monitored to ensure it meets changing needs and conditions. An Adaptive Management Committee, which has met regularly since 2003, is chaired by the City of Burnaby and includes representatives from Metro Vancouver, Stoney Creek Streamkeepers Society, SFU, and SFU Community Trust.

Playground area in Verdant@UniverCity.

64

In addition to exceeding requirements under the SFU Community Trust Green Building Guidelines, Verdant was also designed to meet LEED® Gold certification through energy efficient construction, improved air quality and water conservation measures.

generally avoid. They are in the business of building homes that people can afford and, in that pursuit, they know that buyers, who are often marshaling the last of their resources just to meet the purchase price, will not accept a product that's going to cost them more in the long run to operate and maintain.

Given that the central goal with Verdant was to provide an affordable, entry-level product, the green premium seemed to be out of the question. But, working with Tremain, Vancity came up with an innovative solution. They established a separate "green" mortgage associated exclusively with the operation of the high-efficiency heating and hot water systems. Even though these systems are significantly less expensive to operate, residents agreed to pay the equivalent cost of energy for a traditional building, and the difference was used to pay down the green mortgage. Effectively, this allowed residents to fund the higher upfront capital cost over time.

Another welcome feature of the Verdant development was UniverCity's first small childcare centre, increasingly a necessity as young couples moving into the neighbourhood were beginning to start families. The next critical milestone in the crafting of an actual community came in 2010 with the University Highlands Elementary School. Here, again, was a piece of infrastructure that was, at least on paper, premature. With too few residents to meet the Burnaby School District's normal standard for commissioning a new school, the school was only made possible because the Trust donated an existing SFU building (the former East Academic Annex) and made a large monetary contribution to help refurbish it for its new use. As to the affordability of the Trust's contribution, we regarded this, again, as an occasion when an up front investment was necessary to create a workable community. This stands as a "lesson learned" that would apply equally in a private sector development. The lift in values for the next ten properties to be built exceeded the Trust's investment in the school.

When it came time to do the renovation of the East Academic Annex, the Trust challenged the School District to meet or exceed our green building standards. Indeed, University Highlands became the first LEED® Gold elementary school renovation in British Columbia. According to Russ Sales, who was then the Burnaby School Board Manager of Capital Projects and is now the School Board's Director of Facilities, one of the first and best features that helped the project qualify for LEED® status was the agreement by the City of Burnaby to reduce the usual requirement for a vast swath of pavement next to the school for parking and a car drop-off and pick-up zone. This decision greatly furthers the overall walkability of the UniverCity community design. Almost all students can walk to the school. Many parents drop their children off on their own walk to SFU for classes or work. The decision also reduced the project cost (there was less need for land) and, from a LEED® perspective, Sales says, made it easier to meet goals for managing stormwater.

The list of specific green features that were *added* to the school is also impressive; a radiant heating system fed by a hybrid boiler and supplemented by a hot-air recovery system; a reflective white roof, as well as a green roof and a photovoltaic solar array over the gymnasium; a high-value insulation and low-E glass with advanced light controls and prismatic sensors that make it possible to adjust lighting automatically, in sync with changes in available daylight; low-flush, sensor-activated toilets; no-wax flooring; a monitoring panel in the lobby that allows every student and teacher to track daily — hourly — use of energy and water, a feature that the school uses for its own innovative sustainability curriculum. And more.

We would like to be able to report that the School District expects to save a fortune over the long term and plans to apply all these green solutions in every other upcoming school project. But, Sales says, the truth is more complicated. The School Board faces the same challenge as a first-time home buyer. The Ministry of Education provides a set amount for the construction of a new school, with no credits or additional resources for achieving LEED® standards, and each feature on the LEED® list comes with a 4 percent to 7 percent surcharge, Sales says. He found the resources to make the University Highlands project work, and he continues to apply the most affordable solutions in other projects, but without commitment at every level, it is simply not possible to replicate everywhere what has been possible at UniverCity.

The absence of a parking lot at University Highlands Elementary is mirrored in the community as a whole. Missing is the multi-storey car parkade commonly found in the centre of towns. Parking is a huge consumer of land in the modern city. In Los Angeles, famous for its pavement but far from the worst example, 14 percent of all land is given over to automobile parking. (Even with 3.3 parking spots for every car, somehow there are still few handy places to

> "We would like to be able to report that the school district expects to save a fortune over the long term and plans to apply all these green solutions in every other upcoming school project. But, Sales says, the truth is more complicated."

RUSS SALES, DIRECTOR OF FACILITIES, BURNABY SCHOOLD BOARD

park.) As a commuter campus, SFU has been forced to place a high value on space for parking, so the Trust committed early on that, every time it built over existing parking, it would replace the spots one-for-one. By 2006, that commitment had evolved into a plan to build a six-storey, 1,400-car parkade at the corner of Tower Road and UniverCity High Street, which is, for its location and developability, perhaps the most valuable patch of land in the entire community. In addition, the Trust had committed to the City of Burnaby to provide another, larger childcare centre — a promise it planned to fulfill by building that centre as a penthouse on top of a parkade.

All of this came to my attention in 2006. Michael Geller had announced that he was ready to seek other opportunities and I wound up on the short list of potential replacements as Trust President and CEO. I was incredibly excited by what I saw. I had spent a 30-year career as a planner, development strategist and real estate analyst learning how communities work and how my clients could make them work better. UniverCity looked to me like a magnificent opportunity to perfect the best of what I had learned. And, while it was enticing to be looking at such a broad, open canvas, I was delighted and reassured by the quality — in many instances, the brilliance — of what had been done already.

But the planned parkade gave me heartburn. Some years earlier I had been Director of Business Operations at the University of British Columbia, in which position I was responsible for UBC Parking, as well as UBC's other ancillary businesses. The prospect of building a huge, new multi-storey parkade at UniverCity barely a block from various existing surface parking lots alarmed me.

The first reason was because I had seen the impact of the remarkably successful student transit pass initiative. Beginning in 2003, the regional transit authority, TransLink, agreed to provide every student at UBC and SFU with a reduced-rate monthly pass, which students paid for as part of their tuition and student fees. With their TransLink U-Pass in hand, students abandoned their cars in droves. At UBC, so many students started using transit that daily auto trips to and from the campus fell almost by half, even at a time when the student population was rising dramatically. The same trend was occurring at SFU and the Trust had negotiated to create a similar benefit for new residents at UniverCity (subsidized by Vancity Credit Union's Community Partnership Program), giving rise to some of the highest transit usage rates in all of Metro Vancouver. In that context, it looked to me like the holdouts who continued to drive their cars up and down the mountain would find all the room they needed in the university's existing surface parking lots just south of the High Street.

Working with Heather Tremain, I set out to test that hunch, conducting a survey of parking availability during Convocation week, the busiest period in the academic year. We found that even then, with parents and friends flocking to campus to watch and celebrate their favourite student's graduation, there were empty parking spaces scattered around the campus and UniverCity areas.

Even so, SFU deserves recognition for agreeing to relax the parking requirement. For the past half-century, removing or even just declining to build automobile infrastructure has proved to be one of the most difficult and politicized planning decisions faced at any level. Ultimately, the late Pat Hibbitts, SFU's Vice President Finance, and an invaluable member of the Trust Board of Directors, was convinced by the math. If the Trust had spent the budgeted $79 million on a parking structure, that investment

UniverCity residents
walking home after school.

SOMETIMES SUCCESS COMES FROM WHAT YOU DON'T DO

The project was both obvious and, apparently, unavoidable. We had promised to build a parkade and, as any patient developer might have told you — at any point in the last half century — if you build it, they will come.

But times change, even if it's sometimes hard to see that coming (or to realize that time is leaving you behind). So, in building, budgeting and storytelling, always remember: the most important part is deciding what to leave out. Edit, edit, edit.

Even if your calculations prove incorrect and you find out later that you need to build a certain feature after all, it may still be possible, even if it's more expensive. Build something you don't need — especially, say, a grand, empty eyesore with sloping floors, such as a parking garage, that cannot be converted to any other function — and you will regret it forever.

67

CONSTRUCTION: *Shovels in the Ground*

Not Just Building Buildings — Building Community

SFU Community Trust recognized in its earliest days that Arthur Erickson and Geoffrey Massey's award-winning and distinctive architecture at Simon Fraser University created a legacy that must be both respected and complemented. At the same time, the Trust's mandate was less a challenge to commission greater architecture, and more a command to sponsor great landscape architecture. It was less about the buildings and more about the spaces in between.

A central function of community building is casting great plans not just for how something looks, but how it works. Certainly, the Trust is committed to doing what it can to support architecture of the highest quality and the aesthetic appeal of all of the Trust's buildings is essential. In the words of Norm Hotson, who was instrumental in creating the UniverCity Master Plan and who, for many years, reviewed all design proposals, the Trust has tried to exercise a "definite design vision, with a material palette and a set of colours — a streetscape story." Hotson goes on: "The great places you visit all have this — the collective materials and colours, a certain rhythm and scale to the buildings."

But buildings can't be great if they don't work. You have to get in and out, and, when you stay, you have to be comfortable. In the best case, you should enjoy every part of that process. Buildings must also work together, which sometimes means that an exemplary building takes its beauty from its surroundings as much as its own mass. Equally important are the spaces in between, the streets and sidewalks, the trails and parks, the open spaces and the cloistered niches that create intimate gathering points or dark and dangerous corners, depending on how well they are designed. The places where people gather to live and play comprise the "public realm" (though it would be nice if we could find a more compelling name for this, the most exciting part of the community). In UniverCity the public realm owes a huge debt of gratitude to landscape architect Margot Long and her colleagues at PWL Partnership Landscape Architects, Inc. Without their careful thought and attention, UniverCity simply would not work as well as it does.

Returning to the imposing nature of Erickson's original campus, one of the greatest challenges for the Trust was managing the nexus where town meets gown, where the university and the community meet, overlap, integrate and benefit from one another's presence and influence. There is a brief transition as the dominant east/west axis of Erickson's monolithic campus flows into the UniverCity High Street, and right at that point is an exemplary and award-winning town square that Margot Long designed.

According to Chris Hartman, the Trust's first Director of Development, the square is more than a punctuation point or a formal community gathering place. In the world of community building, Hartman says, "You don't always know what's going to work or why it works." But he knew early on that the town square was going to be a huge success. Hartman says, "Michael (Geller) came in one day, snarling that there were kids swimming in the reflecting pool. I went out and, sure enough, the kids from the childcare centre were all splashing around and cooling off, and I was so pleased. It's great when a public space animates itself, and those kids were having a wonderful time."

View of the Town Square
and SFU campus from The
Cornerstone building.

CONSTRUCTION: *Shovels in the Ground*

UniverCity Childcare
Centre and playground.

TOWARDS SUSTAINABLE COMMUNITIES

This goal can no longer be exotic — or even ambitious. It must attach itself to every project in every village, town or city.

Much as we have tried, UniverCity does not meet the literal definition of "sustainable." Only the UniverCity Childcare Centre is a net zero footprint Living Building. But partly at the urging of Dr. Mark Roseland (author of the book *Towards Sustainable Communities*), we have edged ever closer to that mark. And by reining in energy and water consumption, preserving greenspace and managing stormwater flows, we have come as close to that goal as any community on the planet.

But true sustainability will only be reached when every planner, every designer, every builder and every user fully commits to reducing their own footprints. UniverCity is proud to be leading the way, but equally proud to do so in a manner that makes it as easy as possible for others to catch up.

71

would have come directly out of the profits that would otherwise accrue to the university endowment, money that would be better spent on SFU's core mission of research and teaching. More critically, it would have drained the Trust's operating capital and slowed the pace of development, in a worst case endangering the continuation of the project.

Anyone who has ever run a small organization staffed by smart, ambitious people will know the risks (and, sometimes, benefits) that come with a short-term policy vacuum. In this light I shouldn't have been surprised when, shortly after the decision to abandon the parkade, the Trust's then-manager of Planning and Sustainability, Dale Mikkelsen walked into my office with "a really great idea." Without a parkade, there would be no obvious space for what had been planned as the parkade penthouse childcare centre. Mikkelsen suggested a new site and a new ambition. Our childcare centre could be the first Living Building in Canada.

The Institute's standard comprises 20 Imperatives grouped into seven categories or Petals: Place, Materials, Energy, Water, Health and Happiness, Equity, and Beauty. A builder must meet all of the Imperatives to achieve Living Building certification.

Michael Geller had recruited Mikkelsen as a full-time planner at the Trust, a job for which he was well-qualified, having spent an interesting seven years at the City of Vancouver during a period of growth and change. Mikkelsen says now that, "Geller came to me one day and said that I had been at the City long enough — that I had learned enough to have become useless. He said to me, 'Dale, I'm here to save you.'" Geller was sharply aware that he needed someone with knowledge and passion to look after the sustainability file, and Mikkelsen, who had already invested a great deal of energy in

Resilient And Sustainable

Hardy, sturdy, strong, robust, resistant, flexible and durable: these are all synonyms for resilient, and I'd like to think that they are equally qualities that we have built into UniverCity. From our early champions' first challenges and from the leadership of the SFU Community Trust Board of Directors, we have focused resolutely on the goal of making UniverCity sustainable, but we haven't always made explicit the underlying necessity that, to be sustainable, it absolutely needs to be resilient.

The Rockefeller Foundation's 100 Resilient Cities initiative defines Urban Resilience as:
"the capacity of individuals, communities, institutions, businesses and systems within a city to survive, adapt and grow, no matter what kind of chronic stresses or acute shocks they experience."

That's a tall order. Chronic stresses can include everything from high unemployment or inefficient public transit to endemic violence and chronic shortages of food and water.

Acute shocks include sudden, sharp events — floods, earthquakes, disease outbreaks or terrorist attacks.

Although the purpose was not always made explicit, much of our development approach has been aimed at building resiliency — or preserving the resilient forms that nature demonstrates. The stormwater system was an obvious example, as was the new water supply line that we established to provide redundancy and security to a community that has been relying on a single supply line since 1965.

We also continue to seek resilient options, such as the transit gondola that could safeguard community access in the event that winter storms or accidents close the only road to and from the community.

Regardless, whatever challenges the future holds, we are committed to building a community that can always and easily bounce back.

the International Living Future Institute (then the Cascadia Green Building Council), seemed to him to be the perfect candidate.

For his part, Mikkelsen has always interpreted his job description as "planner in charge of pushing the envelope". He says, "I get to be a nuisance because I have the support to do so. I propose the outlandish and it gets scaled back to the doable." While the idea of creating a Living Building to house the childcare centre was not outlandish, exactly, it wasn't obvious on the day Dale proposed it that it would be doable, either.

The Living Building Challenge standard was developed by the founder and President of the International Living Future Institute, Jason F. McLennan. Unlike the LEED® standard, which offers a set of desirable building components and rewards developers with Platinum, Gold or Silver standing, depending on how many "points" they accrue by incorporating those environmentally benign features, the Living Building Challenge standard challenges builders to create a project with a net zero environmental footprint. Rather than getting credit for adding pre-approved features, builders are encouraged to innovate in whatever way they choose to put up a building that, among other things, generates more energy and captures or recycles more water than its inhabitants consume. Success is measured only after the building is complete and has been operating for 12 months. Instead of assessing the design specifications of energy systems, the International Living Future Institute looks at energy bills to judge performance. The Institute's standard comprises 20 Imperatives grouped into seven categories or Petals: Place, Materials, Energy, Water, Health and Happiness, Equity, and Beauty. A builder must meet all of the Imperatives to achieve Living Building certification.

Working with the SFU Childcare Society, we settled on a new site, one block north of the High Street and about midway between the residential part of the community and the university and transit hub. We chose a team, beginning with the remarkable Karen

Left to right: VP Development, Dale Mikkelsen with HCMA principal Karen Marler, SFU Childcare Society CEO Pat Frouws, and Ledcor Project Manger Bruce Vaserhely in front of the UniverCity Childcare Centre under construction, 2011.

73

GREAT INPUT CAN COME FROM UNEXPECTED SOURCES

It seemed like a lark: a planning charrette tapping the combined wisdom of a bunch of toddlers. But who better to consult if you are trying to design a great building — for a bunch of toddlers!

The UniverCity Childcare Centre project taught us many lessons. As what we anticipate to be the first accredited Living Building in Canada, it taught us to reach and to imagine different ways to do things. Architect Karen Marler stretched beyond the bounds of traditional design and we all found ourselves challenging the best experts for their best advice — and then, sometimes, rejecting it out of hand.

The process, however, is very like any form of consultation: you have to ask. You have to really listen. And, even before a room full of three-to five-year-old children, you have to remember to be humble. Do that, and the decision you make is highly likely to be one to make you proud.

At the UniverCity Childcare Centre design charette, SFU Childcare Society members were encouraged to build and discuss their ideal play environment using modelling clay, 2010.

CONSTRUCTION: *Shovels in the Ground*

Based on the Reggio Emilia System of Learning, the UniverCity Childcare Centre provides unique opportunities both indoors and out for the child to explore water, light, air, gravity, vegetation, and seasonal change.

Marler from the architectural firm HCMA (Hughes Condon Marler Architects). Without the ambition, imagination and determination showed by Mikkelsen, Marler and the construction team at Ledcor, I have little confidence that we could have completed the tasks that followed with anything nearing the same level of success.

The childcare project was sustainable community building in microcosm, a reminder, from consultation to implementation, of the need to apply best practices at every step. We began with a series of workshops, first with internal stakeholders and then with our governmental and regulatory partners. Then we sat down with the clients, a clutch of three- to five-year-olds, and invited them to submit their best ideas. This was the most fun. In the usual design charrette (that is, one involving adults), you're often encouraging people to "think outside the box." Well, preschoolers have no conception that there ever was a box. They were entirely

unrestrained in their creativity. That said, I hope they weren't too disappointed that we didn't wind up with a structure of white tree houses on crooked sticks.

Blue-sky dreaming notwithstanding, we needed to honour the rules of space and scale, access and safety. We were striving to meet the principles of the Reggio Emilia approach to childcare that had been identified from the outset by our partners at the SFU Childcare Society. Parents and professionals in the Reggio Emilia region of Italy designed this preschool philosophy after the Second World War, in the sobering light of the war's devastation and in recognition of the importance of early childhood development. They created a program founded on principles of respect, responsibility, community and a self-guided curriculum, and based on exploration and discovery in a supportive and enriching environment. It was a perfect fit with our goals of sustainable community building.

But we had another challenge — one that I imposed myself when Mikkelsen first raised the childcare alternative. I said, "Sure! We can attempt a Living Building, on the condition that it not cost a dime more than a conventional project. No green premium." That's where the innovations and accommodations from HCMA, Ledcor, and our other partners became so crucial.

As we had seen with Verdant, buildings that are well designed and well equipped from the outset can run more efficiently and more sustainably. If you begin with a structure that is well situated, well insulated and angled to take best advantage of radiant heat from the sun, you reduce the need for heating and lighting hardware, as well as the ongoing expense. We also made a deal with UniverCity's new District Energy Utility to share energy from a rooftop solar-thermal array. This installation generates more thermal energy than the building can use, allowing us to sell the remainder back to the utility, offsetting both costs and the carbon footprint of the electricity that we still need for nighttime lighting.

This example of "scale jumping" illustrates one of the biggest obstacles to positive change. Regulatory authorities and conventional utility partners are generally poorly equipped to deal with innovation. For example, the provincial electrical utility, BC Hydro, has a whole division called Power Smart, dedicated to helping clients conserve energy, thereby reducing the need for the utility to fund expensive capital expansions of its own. The folks at Power Smart loved the childcare project, even offering a grant to help pay for the solar array. But when it came time to hook the new building into the grid, BC Hydro's services division ruled that the centre's energy requirements were insufficient to justify a conventional connection and assessed a connection charge that was larger than the Power Smart grant. Having encouraged us to build a "Power Smart" building, they proposed to penalize us as a poor prospective customer. For the record, it all turned out well in the end. For that, I would like to repeat a personal thanks to then-BC Hydro Chair Bob Elton, who, on learning about the mixed messages coming from his organization, intervened to have our connection charge waived.

The regulatory resistance to change arose again when we began negotiating a water connection. The Living Building Challenge

is to be water independent, to use and reuse only what falls from the sky and to treat any run-off to the satisfaction of the salmon downstream. The Living Building standard forbids the use of noxious chemicals, such as chlorine. Again, senior municipal and health officials expressed admiration for those goals. But the municipal officials, whose job is to enforce the law as written, were unable to approve the re-use of water for potable purposes.

Everyone in Burnaby is mandated by law to use municipally sourced, chlorinated water for drinking, with no exceptions for starry-eyed innovators. When we suggested that our toddler-oriented

We might not have achieved the full goal of building a completely sustainable community yet, but we certainly have developed a model for sustainable practices.

infrastructure would treat and recycle blackwater for use in toilet flushing and irrigation, the regulators declined the application. On that point, however, we ultimately found a compromise, with the regulator supporting water re-use for non-potable purposes, making it possible to link the childcare centre to the raingardens, the underground infiltration fields that are a big part of the award-winning UniverCity stormwater system.

Another obstacle came with the Living Building requirement that no part of the building or grounds include anything that is "red-listed" — that is, construction materials that are suspect for health or environmental reasons. The problem we ran into was suppliers who often couldn't or wouldn't guarantee or even disclose the contents of their products. Sometimes they said these details were proprietary information. Sometimes they admitted that they just didn't know because they incorporated components from other vendors. We finally sent out a complete Red List including substances prohibited by the Living Future Institute, and asked suppliers for a statement confirming that their products contained none of these materials.

All of the foregoing points to two problems for innovators in a fast-paced but heavily regulated world. First, the regulators who often attract so much criticism are the same people who help assure British Columbians the highest life expectancy in Canada (and

UniverCity Bike Park designer Jay Hoots and members of the Norco ride team testing the bike park, 2014.

A Wild Ride In The World Of Non-Traditional Sports Infrastructure

At UniverCity's bike park, 12-year-olds fly off the end of a dirt jump designed by an "expert" who looks like a dreadlocked adrenaline junkie. Depending on your preconceptions, this might seem like the worst idea ever. Or the best. At UniverCity, it's been the best!

The temporary bike park is one of those ideas that might never have come up if not for the fact that the Vice-President Development (Dale Mikkelsen) peddles up the mountain every morning and flies down through the steep dirt tracks at the end of day. We had an empty and already-cleared parcel (24) in the village centre that is slated to be one of the last sites to develop at UniverCity, inspiring Mikkelsen to ask, "Why don't we call Hoots?"

Jay Hoots, of Hoots Inc., designs and builds "non-traditional sports infrastructure," bike parks, trails and pump tracks. In relative terms, bike parks like this are inexpensive to build and they have a very light footprint With the potential exception of a supply of earth that is appropriate and easy to work with, there is nothing to add in construction or take away when you are done. Far from being a place of high risk, the bike park on our last remaining High Street development site has turned out to be a fabulous place for young riders (and, sometimes, their mothers and fathers) to develop their skills before heading (as the youngsters inevitably will) into the labyrinth of challenging trails that lace the Burnaby mountainside.

The park includes three lanes of dirt jumps, a beginner "roller line," and the pump track.* It's clearly well loved in the community. Close to the childcare centre and elementary school, it's busy with the younger set in the daytime and the higher-flying older teens and SFU students in the later evening. So, while it seemed like a great piece of transitional infrastructure, an amenity for young residents that would fill a gap until another permanent park is developed in the coming Slopes neighbourhood, the Trust is now contemplating whether it might be able to find the bike park a permanent home.

*A pump track is a continuous loop of dirt berms and "rollers" (smooth dirt mounds) that you ride without pedaling. The name "pump track" comes from the pumping motion used by the rider's upper and lower body as they ride around the track. ... Pump tracks can be ridden by cyclists of all ages and skill levels.

among the highest in the world). Few public initiatives have saved more lives than the provision of chlorinated water. We seldom find ourselves faced with obtuse, unreasonable people, faceless bureaucrats who punch a clock and then sit at a desk ignoring anything that isn't easy. We are dealing rather with people who have, themselves, fought to establish some of the best standards on the planet and who are justifiably wary about making exceptions.

Second, as our health and environmental understanding evolves, it's hard to keep up. For example, the Living Building Responsible Industry prerequisite requires the use of wood that carries a Forest Stewardship Council (FSC) certification. This is one of several good certification schemes that promote conscientious forestry practices. But the FSC stamp was not available for beetle-damaged Mountain Pine, which for availability and responsibility was the perfect product. The Mountain pine beetle has been at home in British Columbia forests forever. It was a regional nuisance until climate change allowed a population explosion, as more beetles survived warmer winters only to kill so many trees that astronauts can now witness the damage from the window of the International Space Station. For several years, those trees, while dead, are still structurally sound. If the wood is harvested and used quickly, it serves to sequester carbon for the lifetime of the buildings in question. Left to rot or burn, the same trees will become another source of greenhouse gas emissions. So, we had a sustainable

be obtained from within 15,000 kilometres, that consultants travel no farther than 2,500 kilometres, and that building materials and products must be sourced from within 500 kilometres, for the heaviest materials, and 2,000 kilometres for the lightest. These were hard targets to meet, even in the urbanized Pacific Northwest. They would be easier to achieve around Ontario's Golden Triangle. But for communities in the far north, or even the likes of Fort St. John, Fort McMurray, Flin Flon or Churchill, this restriction could block the chance of ever achieving a Living Building certification.

But bad news can have a good corollary. We had a wonderful time finding local suppliers — especially when it came to things like outdoor play spaces. The Reggio Emilia system honours three teachers: the literal teachers who work with students; the parents who support their education; and the environment in which they learn. Thanks to a number of local artists and artisans, our childcare environment is spectacular.

We also proved that lots of sustainable innovations are both doable and affordable in today's market. Every consultant, every regulator, every contractor and every supplier who joined us on this journey is now better prepared to implement the most advanced solutions wherever they are working. We might not have achieved the full goal of building a completely sustainable community yet, but we certainly have developed a model for sustainable practices.

> The Reggio Emilia system honours three teachers: the literal teachers who work with students; the parents who support their education; and the environment in which they learn. Thanks to a number of local artists and artisans, our childcare environment is spectacular.

As to the childcare centre itself, we are incredibly proud of the result. It's been a hit with the client group and the International Living Future Institute had confirmed by press time that we had achieved five of the six petals on a performance basis. Of course, we still need to reach the sixth, but even the Institute's founder and director McLennan acknowledges that the Living Building Challenge is tough. By way of context, he is fond of saying that if the LEED® Gold standard is analogous to Ride Your Bike to Work Day, the Living Building Challenge is the Tour de France; it's all about proving yourself over the long haul. We knew that when we started and we are still in the race and still on track to celebrate the childcare centre as the first official Living Building in Canada.

solution, but no permission. We finally won approval, but only after proving supply chain continuity in the same way a Crown prosecutor must prove that a critical piece of evidence has been tracked and protected, right up to its day in court.

There was one last hurdle to meet the Living Building Challenge standard, and this one could be crippling for people outside well-serviced manufacturing centres. The International Living Future Institute requires that all sustainable energy technology

It becomes apparent, as the UniverCity story unfolds, that the front-end investment in good-quality infrastructure is something of a

School children walking
along University High Street
through the Town Square.

81

SIZE DOESN'T MATTER; REALLY!

It's been a long and interesting conversation in the offices of SFU Community Trust: what is the optimum population for a small-but-complete community? And while we found many reasons to say that the answer was 10,000, we finally had to admit that we were mostly justifying something we couldn't change; given how many housing units are allowed in our Official Community Plan, 10,000 just happens to be the likely number we will reach at build-out.

But all the rationalizing and case building turned out to be a very good thing. In looking for highly functional towns in that population range, or at successful small university towns, our most important discoveries were the components that make a particular town work at a particular size.

So, worry less about what size is right and more about figuring out what features, services and amenities will be right for your size.

82

Heading home from school.

Rendering of the future Corix Biomass Energy Centre to serve SFU and UniverCity residents with green energy beginning in 2019.

theme. It arises once more in the construction of the community's District Energy Utility, mentioned previously. This is one of those everything-that's-old-is-new-again innovations. District energy utilities were once commonplace providers of heat and hot water, especially in commercial buildings in dense downtown cores. For example, Vancouver's Creative Energy (formerly Central Heat Distribution) delivers steam heat to more than 200 buildings, and has been around since the early 1960s. Today, as people seek energy- and cost-efficient alternatives to conventional hydro, gas and oil, steam utilities are enjoying a revival and are spreading more often to residential applications.

A typical district energy system consists of a central plant, an underground distribution piping system, and a series of energy transfer stations in the buildings they serve. In conventional energy applications, BC Hydro or the natural gas distributor FortisBC delivers raw fuel, requiring each individual customer to purchase and maintain further infrastructure to convert fuel to heat or hot water (for example, baseboard heaters or furnaces, hot-water heaters and storage tanks). District energy systems centralize the energy conversion function, removing the need for every condo or every building to buy and maintain these items, thereby reducing both total capital investment and long-term operating costs. With an integrated district energy system, you can also have greater

83

UniverCity Childcare Centre kids playing with the *Woven Huts* designed by Alistair Heseltine.

84

With a High Street, a school, a childcare centre, and an array of sustainable services, the residents who had made an early investment in a home on the mountain were becoming ever more convinced that they had done just the right thing.

flexibility in choosing the most affordable and/or environmentally responsible energy source, whether conventional (natural gas) or alternative and renewable (biomass, heat recovered from sewers or data centres, and geothermal or GeoExchange), and these sources can be changed with a single retrofit if the current one becomes unaffordable or impractical.

UniverCity's system, which was built and is being operated by Corix Utilities, now serves every building that came onstream since 2012, and will serve every new building in the future. Thanks to a $4.7 million grant from the BC government, it is also ready to hook into SFU's heating system, which is currently fired by aging natural gas boilers and is responsible for 85 percent of the university's greenhouse gas emissions. Our system is also running on a natural gas boiler, but it's brand new and high efficiency. By 2019, we expect to have in place a 150-megawatt renewable energy plant fired by wood waste that would otherwise wind up in the landfill. That plant will enable us to remove 11,000 tonnes of greenhouse gas emissions, and, if we choose a combined heat and power model, it may also be sufficient to generate 36 megawatts of electrical energy, enough to supply more than 90 percent of the total annual energy needs for SFU and UniverCity combined.

Best of all, for those who must pay the bill for these services, the utility is regulated by the BC Utilities Commission on a cost-of-service model, which will protect customers in perpetuity from any unnecessary or unfair price increases. As with the Verdant geo-exchange infrastructure, the capital cost of utility infrastructure is being amortized over a period sufficient to keep current energy costs competitive and, as with Verdant, once the front-end costs

are paid off, UniverCity residents can expect to enjoy significant savings compared to off-mountain condominium owners paying for the inefficiency of baseboard heating systems and distributed hot-water infrastructure.

Another benefit of the District Energy Utility is the quality of the system. To quote Kristie Marsden, the then sales manager for Porte Communities, which built two of the first residential buildings to be served by the utility, the hydronic, in-floor radiant heating is "the best kind" — warm, consistent, easily controlled and, unlike forced-air systems, dust free.

The last word on this first phase of construction and on the ambition for the ongoing community is liveability. With a High Street, a school, a childcare centre, and an array of sustainable services, the residents who had made an early investment in a home on the mountain were becoming ever more convinced that they had done just the right thing.

TIMING: WHEN DO YOU NEED WHAT YOU WANT?

Architects, engineers, and construction coordinators all understand the importance of timing. Whether you are laying out a work plan or trying to make sure that materials are on hand when they are needed, timing rules.

But the clock is no less important when it comes to getting the right project into the right location at the right time. The construction world is full of stories of buildings that arrived too late, and failed, or came too soon, and bankrupted their owner (leaving some scavenger to make a fortune when the opportune moment finally arrived).

In Master Planned developments, such as UniverCity, timing can be a complex puzzle. But in every project there will be timing considerations. And in every project, it's worth taking the time to figure them out.

CONSTRUCTION: *Shovels in the Ground*

Devon Knowles' *Near as Far as Far as Near* banners are part of the UniverCity ARTWalk public art program.

Don't Take No For An Answer

This is the kind of advice you don't want to be heard passing around; your employees or your children might take it seriously. But doing something great often means doing something differently. And on most occasions, in the development business, there will always be a platoon of cautious investors and risk-averse regulators who will tell you to park your ambition and go with the tried and true.

Don't listen. Or listen, humbly, and then do the right thing. It might not be easy, but it's likely to work out.

PLANNING A COMMUNITY THAT CAN "REPAIR THE WORLD AROUND IT"

How do you "scale up"? How do you go from the relative triumph of developing Canada's first Living Building — the UniverCity Childcare Centre — to creating a complete Living Community? Christopher Alexander et. al. set a high bar in the revolutionary 1977 design text, *A Pattern Language*: it's a lot to imagine that we might "repair the world." But we surely have a responsibility and, at UniverCity, a legitimate opportunity to create a community that adds to the world's sustainability bounty — and net equity — rather than merely consuming its resources.

That was the task we seized upon in 2012, working with the International Living Future Institute on its Living Community Challenge Pilot, which the Institute described as an effort "to create actionable neighborhood-scale plans for (a) transformative vision of a Living Future (socially just, culturally rich, and ecologically restorative)." Thanks to funding from The Summit Foundation, the ILFI worked on three pilots: ours at UniverCity and one each in Bend, Oregon and San Francisco, California.

At UniverCity, we found two general challenges — and two ways to focus on our overarching goal of building a model sustainable community. The first was to build a community that would serve every inhabitant, and on this, we took inspiration from the late Birmingham University Professor of Geriatric Medicine, Bernard Isaacs. One of the United Kingdom's leading innovators in what was then an emerging field, Dr. Isaacs once said, "Design for the young and you exclude the old. Design for the old and you include everyone." Indeed, a community that is safe and supportive for the frail elderly is going to be safe for all. For example, if streets, parks and services are accessible to wheelchairs and walkers, they will be equally welcome to parents with strollers. Turning that nostrum around — assuming that a community that works for the very youngest inhabitants will also accommodate the eldest (and everyone in between) — the ILFI team created a Living Community Pattern Language that is specifically child-centred, and then applied that language to the existing UniverCity development. The Child-Centered Pattern plan serves as a challenge — and an inspiration — for SFU Community Trust as we work to complete the community over the next decade.

The second area of focus is infrastructure, more mundane, perhaps, but also more foundational. And it revealed some of the reasons why the Trust was successful in developing the UniverCity Childcare Centre as an affordable net zero footprint demonstration project: it's all about scale. As Vice President of Development Dale Mikkelsen points out, it's incredibly difficult, and often prohibitively expensive, to build sustainable buildings one at a time. For example, if you are trying to capture, store, use and recycle stormwater — including blackwater filtered on-site — it is almost impossible in an urban environment where all the neighbouring buildings sit on a hardscape and flush their effluent directly into conventional sewage and storm-sewage systems. But UniverCity already had an innovative stormwater management program to which the childcare centre could connect. It also had a new district energy system into which the solar-powered childcare centre could feed excess energy in the daytime in return for a periodic energy lift when needed after dark. Perhaps most critically, UniverCity also had the trust of the City of Burnaby and other health and safety regulators, so it could innovate at the community level.

This insight offers a significant degree of promise for others who want to build sustainable communities. If you get the right kind of major infrastructure in place, the rest becomes a great deal easier and more affordable for everyone. As Mikkelsen says, "As long as developers can hook into stormwater, sewer and energy connections, they don't have to care about where the stuff goes, or where the energy comes from; they just have

> "This is a fundamental view of the world. It says that when you build a thing you cannot merely build that thing in isolation, but you must also repair the world around it, and within it, so that the larger world at that one place becomes more coherent, and more whole; and the thing which you make takes its place in the web of nature, as you make it."

CHRISTOPHER ALEXANDER ET. AL. IN *A PATTERN LANGUAGE*

to build buildings. You can build a market-scale sustainable neighbourhood for no (additional) incremental cost." Similarly, Mikkelsen advocates that you can pre-vet a materials list to identify the best choices in locally available products that meet sustainability goals. At UniverCity, for example, one of the challenges for developers eyeing the Living Building Challenge, or even just the LEED® performance goals, was to source competitively priced drywall from within a 500-kilometre service area. Finding the right supplier added time and hassle, but if developers all have access to a pre-vetted list of materials and products, it saves time (and therefore money), and the result is positive all around.

When it comes to improving environmental performance, our experience with all of our developers has been extremely positive. They just want clarity and transparency. They want to know what the requirements are and to be sure that all of their competitors are being held to the same standard. Then, they work their hearts out to deliver great products. Our developers have risen to every challenge we've thrown at them and, as a consequence, they have been a big part of our success.

Student at the UniverCity Childcare Centre.

91

CONSTRUCTION: *Shovels in the Ground*

Stormwater Management
Pond at UniverCity

BUILDING COMMUNITY: *Defining, Designing, Developing UniverCity*

3: REFLECTION

What Works; And What Can We Make Better?

It is important, in the living of a good life, to stop once in a while to celebrate your successes. But it is equally important, in those moments of reflection, to ask whether there are things you could be doing better. When I joined the Trust in January of 2007 as President and CEO, it certainly seemed relevant to celebrate the successes of my predecessor, Michael Geller, and everyone else who had made a critical contribution to that point, from Gordon Shrum, Arthur Erickson and Geoff Massey in 1963, to John Stubbs, Jim Moodie, Norm Hotson and David Gillanders in later years. But, just as we had come to revisit the need for a car parkade, we saw a need to adjust to other circumstances that had evolved along the way. So, we embarked on a major reassessment of what had been accomplished to date, what had changed and what still needed to change to give us the best chance of creating a community that complements SFU, improves the lives of its students, staff and faculty, raises revenue for its research and teaching, and offers the world a model of excellence in sustainable practice and planning.

It quickly became evident that the project as a whole would benefit enormously from rezoning to change some of the fundamental assumptions that were embedded in the Official Community Plan and the City of Burnaby's existing zoning bylaw.

The first change was driven by the presence of an actual resident population. David Gillanders and the Trust board had always understood the importance of being open to input from people outside the circle of planning experts. Wisdom really does come from crowds; that's why the university set up a Community Advisory Committee with the original Burnaby Mountain Community Corporation. But there is a stark difference between people from neighbouring communities who might take an interest, and people who actually get out of bed and walk, drive, shop and play on and around the streets, sidewalks, parks and walking trails of a nascent UniverCity community. As you would learn from any former city councillor in any community a simple issue like a missed garbage pickup is minor in theory, but urgently annoying if it's your garbage that's been left in the street, knocked over, and scattered by the ravens or the bears.

Accordingly, as people began to move into the neighbourhood, the Trust worked to recruit the first willing residents to the SFU Community Association and has since conducted regular public opinion surveys through the Mustel Group. It's gratifying that those polls have shown consistently that more than 90 percent of UniverCity residents would recommend life at UniverCity to friends and other prospective neighbours. But some interesting, actionable findings came from questions we might not have thought to ask.

For example, the first round of home sales attracted a lot of young couples that, in the normal course of things, were transforming themselves into young families. By 2007, 20 percent of UniverCity households had at least one child and by 2017 those with children reached nearly 40 percent, closing in on the Metro Vancouver average of 48 percent even though UniverCity has none of the detached homes that families are said to prefer. The trend produced an enthusiastic lobby for homes that were larger and more "family oriented" even if not in the conventional single-family format. Residents and would-be residents were asking for bigger units with more bedrooms, ground orientation, and a garage or other easily accessible storage spaces.

...the first round of home sales attracted a lot of young couples that, in the normal course of things, were transforming themselves into young families.

At the same time, we were noticing a strong demand for compact units close to campus of a sort that would be attractive to students. The Trust's approach on this issue had been on the record since the first formal plan for the East Neighbourhood, which read, "While there will not be conventional student housing, there will be housing for students. Developers will be encouraged to provide

Lunchtime on the High Street.

REFLECTION: *What Works; and What Can We Make Better?*

secondary suites and housekeeping units in townhouses and apartment developments." One of UniverCity's best innovations in this regard was the "flex suite." These are suites within suites that include their own bathroom and kitchen, and can be accessed independently and locked off from the main unit. They are perfect for students, guests or relatives and they work as "mortgage helpers" for young couples who need the income assistance when they first get into the market and prefer to use the extra space themselves when they begin to have children. Even with these units, however, the demand for student-appropriate space was large and growing.

Finally, we found that people were beginning to think differently about the potential for taller towers in the High Street neighbourhood. From an aesthetic and design perspective, it usually makes sense to put the tallest buildings at the highest point of land, as we came to believe should be the case at UniverCity. Such strategically placed towers make the most of high-value views without blocking the views for anyone else. And the outlook from the top of Burnaby Mountain is breathtaking, no matter which direction you are facing. It also makes sense to put the highest concentration of population nearest commercial and transportation services, and the places of work. We began also to hear support for increased building heights among the planners and councillors at Burnaby City Hall. Given the number of national and international planning and city-building awards that UniverCity was attracting to the City of Burnaby, it became more acceptable to contemplate development features that could be viewed from off the mountain because it was so evident that UniverCity was being seen in a good light.

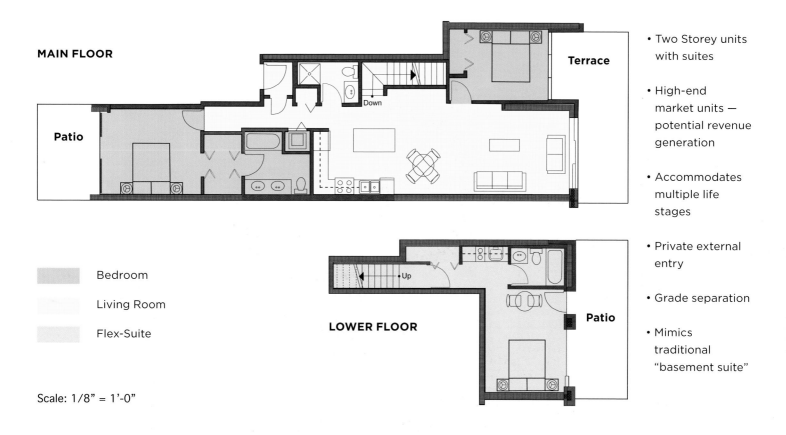

MAIN FLOOR

Patio

Terrace

Down

Bedroom

Living Room

Flex-Suite

Scale: 1/8" = 1'-0"

LOWER FLOOR

Up

Patio

- Two Storey units with suites

- High-end market units — potential revenue generation

- Accommodates multiple life stages

- Private external entry

- Grade separation

- Mimics traditional "basement suite"

LEFT: **Entrance to a flex suite at One University Crescent building.** ABOVE: **Floor plan of flex suite.**

So, one of the major rezoning changes was to shift allowable density. The City of Burnaby agreed that if the Trust lowered density in what is now known as the Slopes neighbourhood, building fewer, larger units to meet the demand for family-oriented homes, it could transfer that density allowance, increasing the unit-count in the High Street neighbourhood. In the process, the City also agreed to raise the cap on building heights from 10 to 20 storeys.

The other reality that is reflected here — and the other rationale for consolidating units in the centre of the community — is that some of the land in the south and southwest of campus might never be developed. Much of the south neighbourhood is so steep and so wet that it could be prohibitively expensive to build on, and difficult to avoid adverse environmental impacts. As for the parcels that lie southwest of the campus, they stand far enough away from the commercial and social core of UniverCity that they may ultimately prove better suited for university purposes than as distant satellites of a pedestrian-oriented UniverCity. Again, it makes so much more sense to concentrate development on a smaller, more-accessible footprint especially when great care is being taken to ensure that this populous area also has all of the parks, trails, open spaces and civic infrastructure (including an elementary school and two childcare centres) necessary to support liveability.

Adding together the elements of the rezoning, UniverCity wound up with a greater variety of building typologies, a more varied and interesting skyline, a better selection of unit types and sizes and,

Spanning an entire block in the heart of the High Street neighbourhood, the architecture is arranged in two primary structures to complement densities and uses while creating connections and view corridors between them.

potentially, a footprint even smaller than the 65 hectares that was identified and allowed in the original Official Community Plan.

Another feature of the rezoning, which was passed in 2010, was the first comprehensive green zoning bylaw anywhere in Canada. The bylaw demonstrated the increased confidence the Trust was experiencing in its ability to deliver a more sustainable product. While the first green building guidelines were introduced carefully and with some concern as to whether developers would or could meet higher standards, it was obvious by 2007 that developers could exceed the performance level we were urging, and obvious as well that buyers were appreciating the green option.

So, to protect buyers and to demonstrate the Trust's commitment to meeting the highest environmental standards, we worked with the City of Burnaby to embed the higher standards in the by-law, making them not just guidelines, but requirements. As Vice President Development Dale Mikkelsen puts it, "The green building demands began as guidelines and Trust-driven requirements. By embedding those requirements in a zoning bylaw, we could demand more up front and administer them more effectively. We can try out different systems and best practices" and because the Trust is the enforcement agency, "the municipality is not risking anything" in that nothing winds up serving as a troublesome precedent. As a result, it became mandatory in all subsequent phases of development that new construction outperform the national Model National Energy Code for Buildings (MNECB) by at least 30 percent for energy efficiency and 40 percent for water efficiency. The first iteration of the bylaw also gave the Trust authority to give a 10 percent density bonus to any developer willing to improve upon that performance or come up with creative and attractive options for stormwater management. Developers responded so positively that both the higher standard and the density bonus are now part of the standard leasing agreement.

There has been ample evidence since then that the bylaw has had the desired effect. The first parcel leased under the new rules was developed by Porte Homes, a 75-unit building called Origin that was so successful that Porte went on to snap up the next available property for the 50-unit project, Lift. Porte Sales Manager at the time, Kristie Marsden says the green standard was part of their success. "We get two kinds of buyers," Marsden said at the time. "Some people are on a mission: they're only going to purchase a

Defining Density

Planners use the term "density" to describe how many people live in a square block or a neighbourhood. This is usually described in terms of a "floor-area ratio," or FAR.

The first UniverCity bylaw decreed that the average FAR would be 1.7, which is to say that for every square metre of land in a particular parcel, development would be limited to 1.7 square metres of residential space.

The City of Burnaby, the planning authority on Burnaby Mountain, has since agreed that the Trust can develop a taller, denser "downtown" in Phase 3, with an FAR of up to 2.2, in return for the Trust's commitment to build a much lower-density Phase 4, so the ground- and family-oriented units in the Slopes will have an overall FAR of 1.1, all the while maintaining an overall community FAR of 1.7.

WHAT IS FAR?

FAR = Floor Area Ration:
The amount of buildable floor area as ratio to total site area.
FAR x Site Area = Floor Area Ratio

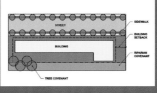

TYPICAL UNIVERCITY DEVELOPMENT SITE
Site Area: 35,000 sq. ft.
Density: 1.0 FAR
Max Height: 4 Storeys
Max Units: 45 Units
Setbacks: 7 Metres
Riparian Covenant: 9,000 sq. ft.
Tree Covenant: 2,500 sq. ft.

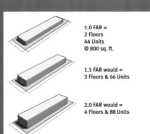

1.0 FAR =
2 Floors
44 Units
@ 800 sq. ft.

1.5 FAR would =
3 Floors & 66 Units

2.0 FAR would =
4 Floors & 88 Units

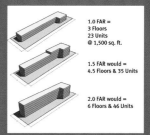

1.0 FAR =
3 Floors
23 Units
@ 1,500 sq. ft.

1.5 FAR would =
4.5 Floors & 35 Units

2.0 FAR would =
6 Floors & 46 Units

Lift in the Slopes neighbourhood, designed as a terraced hillside community, featuring low-rise predominantly wood-frame homes for families.

home built to the highest green standard. Others are looking here because they like the community, and they're pleasantly surprised to find the homes are so sustainable". The high standard became a differentiator, drawing buyers back to Burnaby Mountain.

Bearing in mind, as well, SFU's original ambition that UniverCity should be a model of good practice, it was gratifying in 2015 when the National Energy Code for Buildings was updated to catch up to our higher standard. And SFU Community Trust remains committed to exceeding even those requirements, continuing to pioneer on the road to sustainability.

Regardless of whether UniverCity is trying to influence the industry standard in some particular criteria, it is always good to keep in mind that we are participating in a highly competitive market. It's a factor you might forget when the market is as strong as it was in the early to mid-2000s. When I arrived at the Trust in January 2007, I found an organization that was disciplined and appropriately lean. There were no obvious signs that we should be retrenching, looking for efficiencies or slowing down what had been an orderly pace of development.

Yet, by that same summer, everyone in the development industry was looking for a place to hide. Driven to the brink by the questionable promotion and securitization of subprime mortgages, the United States' real estate bubble burst, bankrupting some of the oldest financial institutions on the continent and upending prospects for the whole world economy. Canada fared better than the United States, and the robust Vancouver housing market sputtered, but didn't stall, avoiding the losses or setbacks that were typical south of the border. But you could still smell panic in many of the country's bank boardrooms and development offices.

How nice, then, to be reporting to a Board of Directors with the depth of experience and the calm leadership evinced by people like Chair David Gillanders, as well as real estate and finance industry professionals including Bruno Wall, Daniel Pekarsky, Howard Nemtin, Peter Ng and Barry Macdonald. Along with the always-composed late SFU Vice President Finance, Pat Hibbitts, these and other Board members took a breath and agreed to stay the course, continuing to plan and invest in an expanding community. "We didn't sell any parcels in 2008-09," David Gillanders says now. "We thought the downturn was a blip so we just took the properties off

101

CULTIVATE PATIENCE: IT'S TIME'S GREAT ADVERSARY

In the development business, time is money. It costs money to buy land, to hold land, to prepare land. You can spend a fortune in planning costs while appealing to City councils for zoning and development approvals. And even after gaining permissions, you still must build and sell your product. Only at the end of the process might there be a payday.

Yet nothing pays a bigger dividend than patience. If you have the resources — and the steely nerve — to buy in bad times, to hold or build while the market is soft (and the trades are readily available) and then to wait till the market is hot before you sell, you can maximize your gain. But few are in that position.

Still, if you cannot afford patience outright, choose deliberation. Nothing is more costly than an unforced error. Even if you can't take all the time you want, be sure to take all the time you need.

Residents enjoying a game of chess in the Town Square.

the market. But the office kept running flat-out. It left more time for planning, less time overseeing sales."

This approach worked out well on a couple of counts. First, as Gillanders says, "four or five projects were just beginning construction, so it didn't look like nothing was happening." Second, by the time the Trust was ready to release new parcels for lease, "the market had come back higher."

One project that proceeded apace was the second mixed-use, commercial-residential building on the High Street, which the Trust contracted with Liberty Homes to build. The Hub was designed to complement UniverCity's first commercial building, The Cornerstone, and to provide space on completion for the grocery store that, with the elementary school, remained the most crucial missing ingredients in the still-emerging community. Thus, in 2010, just as the economy was getting back on track, Nesters opened a full-service grocery store, making it possible for the first time to live on the mountain without having to make frequent pilgrimages into Burnaby in search of provisions for the day-to-day.

Left to right: Buy Low Foods President Dan Bregg, SFU Community Trust CEO Gordon Harris, City of Burnaby Mayor Derek Corrigan, Nesters Market store manager Eric Olson, and Overwaitea Food Group's Moreno Trevisan at the grant opening of Nesters Market, 2010.

Depending on your corporate preferences and your beverage of choice, the culminating commercial installations might either be the Starbucks or the liquor store, which were both welcomed in 2016. The latter stands as one of those points of collaboration that exemplify what is possible when partners stand on principle, but work together for the community's benefit. The liquor store had sat for some time on the list of desired mountain services, but it came (or at first, didn't come) with complications. The university wanted the clearest assurance that the community would introduce a responsible vendor and the City of Burnaby was equally firm that any outlet be unionized. Practically speaking, that meant it had to be a BC government liquor store, but government policy mandates that any store operation smaller than 6,000 square feet should be let to the private sector, and UniverCity needed something about half that size. The solution came from former BC Minister of Justice

Suzanne Anton, a long-time advocate and champion of the best aspects of development at UniverCity. Under her leadership, Anton's Ministry ultimately agreed to an exception to the square-footage rule, and the community now has a unionized, reliably responsible, smaller-footprint BC government liquor store, yet one more reason to forego even a weekend trip off the mountain.

In reflecting on where we have come, and in thinking about the community that we have carved out of the forest and the respect that we have shown in the process, it's important to consider the other symbiotic relationships and partnerships that have made our journey a success. These partners include developers, financiers, experts and academics, dreamers who pushed us to do more, and regulators who made sure we did it with discipline and high standards. Prominent, perhaps even pre-eminent on the list of partners, has been the City of Burnaby.

UniverCity's first Development Manager, Chris Hartman, who, in the early days of tree cutting and road-building could be heard, frequently, snarling about anyone whose intervention was slowing his pace, has only praise today for the relationship. "Burnaby

103

Banking On Great Partners

In 2009, just as the Trust's contractor/partner Liberty Homes announced that it was 21 days from substantial completion of our new building, The Hub, we learned that, because of the economic downturn and international financial crisis, our bank had decided to cancel all lending on commercial real estate. We thus had less than three weeks to negotiate a $14-million mortgage with an institution that had no previous experience dealing with the SFU Community Trust.

It happened that a member of the Trust Board had been talking to Canadian Western Bank on another account and suggested we make contact. We did so, and CWB President Ken Pollock immediately jumped on a plane from Edmonton and flew out to look at the project. And, with thanks to Liberty for a very short extension, we were there with the money within 24 days — a turnaround time that most people in commercial lending would describe as impossible.

The Trust was incredibly grateful on that occasion and has been delighted since with the continuing high level of great service that we have received from Canadian Western Bank.

staff were directly involved at every step — and they added value," Hartman says. "They took ownership of the community. If something went well — or something went badly — they took it personally. They had the same level of involvement as any of us."

Beginning with significant praise for Robert Renger, who was the lead planner, Hartman goes on, "But the (Burnaby City) planning directors, Tony Parr and Jack Belhouse, really set the culture. When creativity was necessary, it was Belhouse who got the engineers to compromise."

Among the early keys to success were the frequent meetings, often booked long before a specific proposal was on the table. Hartman says, "We would often get together informally, with agendas and

titles left at the door, and talk even when there was no actual application in front of the city. It allowed us to talk as members of a group who were all interested in moving the process forward." Their conversations were sometimes reported to be "free and frank," which is to say, loud and inconclusive. There are stories of meetings that ended with a scowl, a sniff, an unscheduled early exit, and even the slamming of a door. But Hartman says there was always a font of goodwill. He says that, regardless of periodic disagreements, Burnaby city staffers "were always attentive and available to us."

Robert Renger remembers it much the same way: "The Trust was as enthusiastic as we are about creating facilities of the highest standard. And Geller was very creative. He very literally built off the Community Plan; he didn't fight it." In his 33 years at the City of Burnaby — he retired in 2015 — Renger says that working on UniverCity "was definitely the high point of my career."

Part of our success arose from the Trust's composition and its function of leasing property on behalf of Simon Fraser University. On occasions when we at the Trust were trying to push the envelope, to raise standards or be more innovative than the engineers might at first appreciate, Renger says, "We were better able to trust the Trust. Because they were leasing the land, we knew that they were going to have to live with the consequences of what they did. They would be involved forever. Not like a developer who finishes and walks away."

Burnaby Mayor Derek Corrigan makes the same point. Having been first elected as a City councilor in 1987, Corrigan was around throughout the bumpy early negotiations. And while he was skeptical at the outset, he looks back enthusiastically today. More than a partnership, Corrigan suggests that the City and the Trust have enjoyed a peer relationship. Both entities were created by government, with each ceding some of its own authority to the other. And if the City had a higher degree of "trust in the Trust," it also had higher expectations, the Mayor says. "We challenged SFU to do more than any other developer. There was an obligation for the university to set an example and achieve goals that others can't." In Corrigan's eyes, UniverCity was, and remains, "an experimental laboratory." The City "trusted Geller and Harris to be constantly looking for ways to balance social, economic and environmental goals, and they accomplished that in spades."

> "We challenged SFU to do more than any other developer. There was an obligation for the university to set an example and achieve goals that others can't."

DEREK CORRIGAN , BURNABY MAYOR

That good partnership has also helped the Trust achieve one of its principal goals, to be a model of good practice. Corrigan says, "It's hard to ask developers for innovation." They're working on tight schedules and any changes that might cause delays or add costs frighten off their financiers. But when UniverCity demanded, for instance, that every developer on the mountain exceed the national building code standards for energy and water efficiency, Corrigan says, "It set an example that you can now demand of developers. You can point to SFU meeting this standard and making money, and you can say, 'Don't be scared. It can be done.'"

Just as Burnaby and SFU share an interest in good urban planning, Mayor Corrigan says the two are equally committed to the success of the university itself. He says that Burnaby is "a leader among so-called second-tier cities — Helsinki, Barcelona, Dublin, Munich," and that's tied very closely to the city's emerging success as a centre of high-technology innovation, with the establishment of companies such as Electronic Arts and Ballard Power Systems. Corrigan says SFU is crucial to that trend: "There's an international competition now to attract creative industries, but the best strategy is not to attract, but to develop. The key to that strategy is to have great educational institutions so you can be an initiator. You have a better chance of keeping a business that started in your city than of attracting one from away."

That recognition indicates a level of engagement that pleases current SFU President Andrew Petter. SFU's close connection to community was one of the factors that drew Petter to the position of President in the first place and was a focus of the strategic visioning exercise that he ran on assuming the presidency. In 2010, his vision set a challenge for SFU to be "Canada's most community engaged research university." To that end, Petter says, UniverCity has been a huge boon.

GOOD PARTNERS MAKE GOOD PROJECTS: I

It is tempting to imagine, as the development overseer in a Master Planned community, that SFU Community Trust had a right to claim a great part of UniverCity's success. In fact: our partners did it.

We have been incredibly fortunate to work with a group of world-class developers who consistently accepted our challenge to build to higher-than-market environmental and construction targets and then outperformed our expectations.

We collaborated with subject-area experts like Heather Tremain, and with financiers such as Vancity Enterprise, who also worked together to produce one of our most successful condo projects. We found partners in the Burnaby School District and in the SFU Childcare Society, who helped us bring excellent and environmentally innovative care and elementary education to the mountain.

So, your best successes may come not from what you do, but from who you do it with. So, search for great partners; and be sure to credit them for their contribution.

REFLECTION: *What Works; and What Can We Make Better?*

GOOD PARTNERS MAKE GOOD PROJECTS: II

A good jack-of-all-trades can do everything. But a great jack-of-all-trades won't.

We all have strengths and weaknesses. We all have specific expertise and our best chance of success, individually and organizationally, usually comes from understanding what we do well, and contracting the rest out to professionals.

SFU Community Trust certainly had the administrative capacity to operate a district energy utility. There's just no evidence that we had the capacity to do it well, especially compared to an organization like Corix Utilities that specializes in the field.

So, when you are straying outside your core competency, find the right professional for the job and negotiate the best deal you can. You, your partner and your customers/clients/stakeholders/debtholders are likely to be much happier in the long run.

From its earliest days, when it emerged as the so-called *Radical Campus*, SFU's faculty and students always played an activist role in Metro Vancouver. But community engagement became more direct in the 1990s with the establishment of a second campus in downtown Vancouver, and yet more so in the early 2000s as SFU developed a catalyzing third campus in what is now Central Surrey. President Petter is committed to bringing SFU's message off the mountain to engage with and strengthen those other communities, and he sees UniverCity as the perfect plan to bring a community to the mountain. "It was visionary," he says.

It was also both hugely effective and (now) clearly responsible to turn away from the old, suburban, single-family development pattern. Petter says, "It's obvious, looking back, but at the time it was far from obvious and something that, but for the grace of those early decision makers, could have been very destructive." The alternative, this compact, convenient, increasingly sustainable community, has been a blessing for SFU. The university now has an immediate supply of homes for staff and faculty and more places for students to live right next to the campus. As well, Petter says, "We have services, commercial and retail infrastructure, the elementary school and the childcare centre — a sense of a Main Street and a community centre. And with every new facility and service, the university benefits by the presence of the community. And the community benefits by access to the university."

This access is practical and academic. Residents of the community are welcome to use SFU services such as the library and the sport, fitness and recreational facilities, as well as to attend lectures, and other educational and cultural opportunities that are open to the public, everything from plays and presentations to the Starry Night program at the SFU Observatory. The academic overlap runs in two directions. Obviously, there is handy access for students, staff and faculty who work or study at SFU. And there is also a ready opportunity for SFU, "the Engaged University," to engage directly with research opportunities on the mountain. There are cooperative research agreements with the childcare centre and the elementary school, and students in the School of Resource and Environmental Management have conducted numerous research projects in the community and, on occasion, have had direct input into plans and decisions. In all of these connections, President Petter says, you are reminded that, "We are the university that made it our mission to be connected to the community."

SFU Chief Facilities Officer Larry Waddell, says, "I don't think people really anticipated the impact on the quality of the student experience and the experience for employees. There is no opportunity for a double-blind experiment, but you can close your eyes and think about what SFU would be like without UniverCity — and it's unthinkable." Waddell also talks about the symbiosis between university and community. "You wind up with critical mass. We're able to justify infrastructure improvements that would not have been affordable for the university alone, and the benefit of two markets — residents and students — that become sufficient to support services such as the grocery store. Richard Bolton Park and the Town Square are also tremendous resources that benefit SFU way more than the community."

That said, President Petter notes that the direct economic benefits to SFU have been slower in coming, in part because of how the Trust has approached its responsibilities and, inevitably, because so much of the development investment is loaded to the front end. "But," he acknowledges, "there is already an income stream from the Trust, and it will grow stronger and steadier." The Trust has also built and paid for more than $16 million in hard infrastructure that is of direct service to the university itself, including a new water line that provides double security to the university's supply of fresh water for the first time.

"Still," President Petter concludes, "there is no question that the presence of the community itself is an even greater benefit. It was never just a real estate play, never just a project to derive income. It was not even about trying to expand SFU's services. It's about our sense of self as a university — our purpose, our commitment to building something sustainable and providing lessons from which others may benefit. And on that count, it's been an undeniable success."

Petter's predecessor as president, Michael Stevenson, makes a similar point, "If UniverCity was based primarily on making money for the university it would have been a bad deal." SFU had some guidance in this from the experience at the University of British Columbia, which had started its development process earlier and in a neighbourhood where high existing property values acted to skew the price of new units beyond most people's budget. Perhaps as a result, Stevenson says, "There was a spirited debate about the concerns of equitability. We would have offended the university community to use the project to cream the luxury housing market."

Located next to SFU, community residents are welcome to enjoy many of SFU's cultural, recreational, and educational amenities such as the Trottier Observatory and Science Courtyard.

REFLECTION: *What Works; and What Can We Make Better?*

UniverCity and SFU community members alike gather in the Town Square for food, entertainment, and music.

Still, he says, "People were pretty surprised by how quickly UniverCity prices rose. One of the successes of the project was to boost land value for Burnaby as a whole."

SFU Chancellor and former Trust Board member Anne Giardini, who is the former president of the forestry giant, Weyerhaeuser Company Limited, says, "I came into this position already understanding the notion of 'forests forever.' I knew that trees verge on the magical; well, communities can verge on the magical as well." And in community as in the forest, sustainability is the key. "It's the commitment we make to this generation and to every generation that follows."

On which count, few people are more inclined to look at things through a sustainability lens than the International Living Future Institute's Jason F. McLennan, who says, "The university is, in a sense, healing what was missing — life on the mountain. The

> "I came into this position already understanding the notion of 'forests forever.' I knew that trees verge on the magical; well, communities can verge on the magical as well. It's the commitment we make to this generation and to every generation that follows."
>
> **ANNE GIARDINI, SFU CHANCELLOR & FORMER TRUST BOARD MEMBER**

functioning of the university was entirely based on the automobile; now, people don't have to go down the mountain every day. That, alone, is a victory."

McLennan is kind about according credit to those among us who have been involved in planning and overseeing development on the mountain. He says, "There has been a great team of people who understand planning for the long term." McLennan said specifically that Dale Mikkelsen and I have been "a rare combination." He particularly noted our determination that our successes be replicable, that others can learn from our mistakes and repeat our successes. McLennan also says, kindly, that Dale and I "have been very creative in how they solve problems. I really admire their thinking and their approach." In reflecting on the rarity of our

109

110

A Model Sustainable Community: A Model Master Planned Community

At a time when public agencies are taking increasing leadership as "master developers," UniverCity is worth emulating for more than its aspirations to sustainability, says architect and urban designer Heather Tremain.

As cities, big and small, regenerate, and as public agencies seek to make the best (re-) use of large and valuable blocks of urban land, more and more public institutions are moving into development, Tremain says, citing school districts, health organizations, First Nations and municipalities among those organizations that frequently have redevelopments that are large enough to require master planning at the community level.

In this regard, "The Trust has done almost everything right," says Tremain, who worked in the early days of the project as a consultant and, for a short time, as development manager, and who is now CEO of the Toronto-based Options for Homes Limited. Part of the reason for the Trust's success was its far-sightedness, she says. "As a 1,000-year institution, the university has the capacity to take the long-term view," and because the property is being leased, rather than sold, SFU also has a long-term economic investment.

But Tremain argues that the planning principles that worked for the Trust would work equally well for any developer trying to maximize the value of a large property, because today's buyers are willing to pay a premium to live in a well-planned, walkable and resilient community. "UniverCity has busted the myth that 'green' and 'affordable' are mutually exclusive. That's a legacy that people should notice."

relationship, it's hard to tell who, between Dale and I, was the overreaching provocateur and who the source of calm correction. The record would probably show that we frequently switched roles. Regardless, Dale certainly deserves all of McLennan's praise.

There are many others, at every level, who also deserve praise, but a few cannot be overlooked in any list. The original team, assembled by consultant Jim Moodie, set UniverCity on a firm foundation from the outset. And Robert Renger is generous in crediting the early work and ongoing planning and design input of Hotson Bakker (now Dialog) and especially Norm Hotson. Renger says, "We couldn't have asked for better consultants. The detailed vision got it going very quickly. And Norm Hotson is very, very conscientious." Anne Giardini also points to a leader whose quiet good judgment always made bad days bearable and good days better. She says that long-serving Board Chair "David Gillanders has gone above and beyond. Life's credit is not doled out fairly. David has put in hundreds of thousands of hours only for the pleasure of seeing a job well done."

But without basking too much in praise or self-congratulations, it's worth going back to McLennan for a final word and, perhaps not surprisingly, a challenge. He says, "The university could go much further in the rest of the development, using the childcare centre as a model. There are, now, lots of individual Living Buildings in the world, but by finding a way to hold that standard together through multiple parcels, UniverCity has the ability to be a model." The idea is to scale up the ambition of the Living Building Challenge into a Living Community Challenge. In fact, the International Living Future Institute has already done renderings and written a vision for what a Living Community master plan might look like at UniverCity. And that final word? McLennan says, "My aspiration for them is that they keep raising the bar."

University Highlands Elementary school
musicians performing in the Town Square.

CELEBRATE, CELEBRATE, DANCE TO THE MUSIC!

Life can be stressful. And with big, long-term projects, that stress can build to crippling loads. Yet, just when you should be celebrating the culmination of a huge endeavour, you are, most likely, just digging into a new challenge, building a bigger, better box for a larger stress load to come.

So, celebrate. Call in your partners, your employees, the friends you've been ignoring — perhaps even family members who have missed you through all of this project. Arrange a party. Send invitations — and thank you cards.

Debrief what went wrong, by all means. Reflect. But, no matter what they say about learning from your mistakes, the best results come from refining and repeating best practices — one of which is picking the right time to take a bow, and enjoying the feeling.

113

REFLECTION: *What Works; and What Can We Make Better?*

View from the Origin building.

BUILDING COMMUNITY: *Defining, Designing, Developing UniverCity*

LIVEABILITY
— FROM THE GROUND UP

In 1943, the psychologist Abraham Maslow published his now-famous Theory of Human Motivation, in which he presented what he called a hierarchy of human needs. Essentially, Maslow argued that humans could not hope to achieve the goals of belonging, self-esteem and self-actualization if they had not already taken care of their physiological requirements and guaranteed their safety. You need clean air, fresh water, a decent meal, a warm and comfortable place to sleep, and a free moment when you are not looking over your shoulder in fear or concern before you can start making friends and inspiring people.

The theory has been criticized as simplistic, but it still maps nicely onto the goal of liveability. You can't aspire to building a prosperous, stable, equitable and richly creative community if you don't start with a good sewage system and a robust (and redundant) water supply. You need well-built and resilient homes. You need a grocery store. You need walking paths and streets that even the very young and the very old can manage in comfort and safety. You need all the energy, communication, and transportation infrastructure that make it possible for the citizens of the community to connect and to flourish.

In the 21st century, we also understand that our collective and ongoing security requires that all communities aspire to greater sustainability. We can't count on clean air or a stable and liveable climate — globally or locally — if we don't begin to take responsibility for the impacts of our decisions. In that context, high walkability and easy access to excellent transit becomes more than a matter of convenience; in the long term, it could contribute to human survival.

In laying the groundwork for UniverCity, SFU Community Trust worked first to establish a strong foundation and to test the limits of sustainable planning and practice. Then, having attended to the basic infrastructure, we worked up the hierarchy, for example, by establishing the parks and public places where residents and visitors alike could meet and build a sense of belonging — a sense of community. We chose educational options that inspired confidence in our youngest residents (Maslow's "self-esteem"), and we instituted initiatives, such as our public art program, that signal this as a place where residents may achieve their own goals and, on the best days, contribute to the good of the community as a whole.

In this framework, "liveability" is not a stable endpoint: you can't build "a liveable community" and then ignore its maintenance, any more than you can achieve the highest levels of intellectual accomplishment without attending to the banalities of day-to-day existence. Rather, the goal — "liveability" — is a reminder that great communities must work at every level, starting strong on the ground and reaching, consistently and sustainably, to enable and support the community's highest ambitions.

PUBLIC ART

It takes more than bread, wine, energy efficiency and innovative design to sustain a complete and healthy community. There must also be art and beauty. And while the latter exists in abundance in the natural features of Burnaby Mountain, in what you see in every direction, the Trust has always felt a responsibility to meet that standard in the built environment, to create opportunities for artistic and cultural expression — emotional, engaging and sometimes provocative public statements that this is a community of people who care about the life of the mind and the heart.

The first piece of public art on the mountain came in response to a request — or a provocation — by Professor Mark Winston, then-Director of the Simon Fraser University Semester in Dialogue program. Winston had a cohort of students who were interested in orchestrating an art project, a competition that would be open to SFU faculty, students and alumni. Winston asked if the Trust would commit prize money to finance the work and offer a site for its permanent display. And then-president Michael Geller (while withholding a veto for quality) took the bait.

The resulting work, *Concrete Tree Imprint*, by SFU Alumni Amelia Epp and Kevin Sandgren, is a juxtaposition — both awkward and elegant — of the Burnaby mountaintop's falling forest and the uncompromising concrete being poured in its place. The artists chose three segments of deciduous trees that had been felled to make way for Harmony, the first residential development, and they cast impressions of these segments in concrete cubes, which they then assembled in an off-kilter column. Today, whether you read it as a protest of what was sacrificed in the forest or as a celebration of the human re-expression of nature, you cannot walk past these playful concrete blocks without considering both the conflicts that we have overcome and the resolution that we have wrought in the midst of this new community.

Given, again, the tension inherent in cutting down trees to make way for a "model sustainable community," it might not be surprising that the second UniverCity art project also came out of the forest. SFU Communications Professor and then-Trust Board member Bob Anderson brought Geller a book

One University Crescent. LEFT: **From the UniverCity ARTWalk Public Art program:** *EcoSoMo* by Matthew Soules. RIGHT: *Near as Far as Far as Near* street banners by Devon Knowles.

from the United Kingdom called *One Tree*. It told the story of a grand but dying oak that had been cut down, preserved and distributed among artists who used it to create a variety of different works. Geller loved the idea and agreed to launch a UniverCity version called *Two Trees*, using a maple and a cedar that had been felled in 2003 on what would become the site of The Cornerstone. The trees were kiln dried and cured on the mountain, and pieces were distributed among 27 artists, whose creations were then displayed first at SFU Burnaby and later at the Vancouver Art Gallery in downtown Vancouver.

As a long time champion of the arts in British Columbia, as Chair of Presentation House Gallery, and as a director on boards including the Vancouver Contemporary Art Gallery and the BC Arts Council, I was keen to transform the ad hoc approach to public art, hoping to develop a process that was more formal and official, while still being efficient and inexpensive, such that the bulk of any contribution made to public art went to the artist and their work and not to the process. I also wanted to enshrine a clear mission to use our resources to nurture emerging artists and to support the Four Cornerstones of Sustainability: environment, economy, education, and equity. I was delighted by the response, both from the SFU Community Trust Board and from the development community. The Trust agreed to implement a dollar-a-square-foot charge to developers to support a formal public art program, and Jesse Nobbs-Thiessen from Liberty Homes embraced the challenge of creating the inaugural project, commissioning a remarkable work by the artist and sculptor Erica Stocking. Liberty was building UniverCity's second commercial/residential building, The Hub, and when Stocking came to tour the site, she reported that she was struck by the stark, imposing, but ultimately protective yellow safety fencing surrounding the property. Inspired, she designed a series of *Yellow Fence* gates with increasingly complex grids, evolving down the row of townhome-style entryways.

The work has continued to flourish in all manner of media, from Devon Knowles's lightpost banners (*Near As Far As Far As Near*) and the concrete biers and benches of Matthew Soules's *EcoSoMo* to the delicate metal latticework of Bruce

TOP: *Concrete Tree Imprint* by Amelia Epp and Kevin Sandgren.
BOTTOM: *Rootwad Cedar Climber* by Warren Brubacher.

REFLECTION: *What Works; and What Can We Make Better?*

Voyce's *Nest with Chrome Eggs*. In the two-storey atrium of the CentreBlock building, you will find Holly Ward's *Cosmic Chandelier*, a re-imagining of the constellation Orion, rendered in copper-clad steel pipes and cables, with frosted glass and LED pendants forming the cool, bright "stars" we connect to outline the figure of the hunter/warrior. Orion's nebula is a dense vertical cluster of Plexiglas rods.

The UniverCity public art collection reveals a steady influence of natural materials, even in the artifice of new and frequently very practical works. For example, the UniverCity Childcare Centre, the "greenest childcare centre on the planet," according to International Living Future Institute founder Jason F. McLennan, was an excuse and an inspiration for some robust, hands-on artistic creations. Rather than accept conventional slides and monkey bars, the Trust engaged three artists to design and deliver children's play structures that would be hardy enough to serve their purpose while honouring the ambitions of sustainability inherent in the Living Building Challenge. The results are both beautiful and fun, from the simplicity of Brent Comber's Western Red cedar steps, *Nightswimming*, to Warren Brubacher's Rootwad *Cedar Climber* and Alastair Heseltine's *Woven huts*.

As a testament to the artistic merit of this work, one of Heseltine's *huts* was included in the 2011 Vancouver Art Gallery exhibition, *WE: Vancouver — 12 Manifestos for the City*. It was the only installation welcomed to the show from outside the Vancouver city limits. The inclusion was further complicated by the nature of the hut itself, which is woven from wood and designed for life in the great outdoors. The gallery has a strict and appropriate policy on bringing in organic material that could contain any tiny pest that might wander off and do damage to other works of art, so the Trust was given a choice: before delivery, the hut must be sterilized either by superheating or freezing. Superheating the hut would have left nothing but a pile of ash, so Development VP Dale Mikkelsen went on a successful hunt for a commercial freezer large enough to accommodate the hut. From then, till now, indoors as art or outdoors as playspace, the hut remains a hit. All three of the childcare centre pieces offer treasures to seek and places to hide, and will surely inform and engender a whole new generation of art aficionados.

TOP: *Nightswimming* by Brent Comber.
BOTTOM: *Yellow Fence* by Erica Stocking.

Cosmic Chandelier by Holly Ward.

REFLECTION: *What Works; and What Can We Make Better?*

The UniverCity Childcare Centre opened in 2012. The revolutionary facilitiy with space for 50 three-to-five year olds, is expected to be the first building in Canada to meet the Living Building Challenge.

9075

UniverCity Childcare

A 21ST CENTURY FOOTPRINT — SMALL AND LIGHT

It all started simply enough: in the original concept, a footprint was, literally and narrowly, the mark you left — in sand or snow — when you walked by.

Planners and architects later expanded the definition, using the word metaphorically to describe the imprint of a building: its footprint on the ground. (Landscaping was extra!)

Then, in the early 1990s, a Ph.D. student named Mathis Wackernagel and his supervisor, Dr. William Rees, from SFU's sister institution, the University of British Columbia, coined the term, "ecological footprint" — a measure of human impact on nature. Wackernagel and Rees pointed out that if you cut trees in one place to build a home in another, then the functional impact of the new building spread beyond its strict physical dimensions. Suddenly, in our highly consumptive society, the word footprint could mean anything from the muddy track we left on a beige carpet to the extent of orangutan habitat alienated by our use of palm oil.

But never mind the confusion: at UniverCity, SFU Community Trust has embraced every definition of the term, beginning — crucially — with the physical footprint of the community itself. Given a potential development area of 385 hectares, Simon Fraser University committed to restricting the new community to within a 65-hectare area, donating the remaining land for protection, in perpetuity, as part of the Burnaby Mountain Conservation Area. But even within that smaller footprint, SFU Community Trust has set aside property that is too wet, too steep, too far to be embraced within a walkable community — or simply too valuable as parkland or trails — thereby reducing the buildable footprint by as much as half again.

Then, in a campaign to reduce the community's "carbon footprint" (the total greenhouse gas emissions generated from heat, light, construction or transportation), the Trust constrained development further — choosing energy-efficient building styles and heating technologies, and supporting excellent pedestrian access to public transit. And, of course, in constructing the UniverCity Childcare Centre to a standard worthy of the first Living Building in Canada, the Trust has demonstrated that you can build a structure with a net zero ecological footprint (see page 71).

The point, here and everywhere, is to keep score. Compact, walkable communities, built to preserve greenspace and natural habitat, can improve liveability even as they reduce the human footprint. And, given the anticipated lifecycle of a modern-day building, the long-term implications for environmental dislocation, energy consumption, and increased (or decreased!) transportation needs and costs, reducing the physical and conceptual footprint of all community development presents one of the most far-reaching opportunities to ameliorate human impact and to advance the cause of sustainability.

121

FROM WASTELAND TO WONDERLAND: UNIVERCITY RESIDENTS CELEBRATE A NEW SENSE OF COMMUNITY

An "intellectual industrial park," an "office complex for a community of students and faculty," a "weekend wasteland" — before the development of UniverCity, Simon Fraser University's Burnaby Mountain campus tended to attract bleak descriptions. Students living in SFU residences west of the campus, and SFU presidents who lived in the rather lonely Arthur Erickson-inspired President's Residence east of the campus all reported a rather dismal campus. Universities are supposed to be vibrant and exciting, full of life and learning. During the week, SFU was all of that and more. As mentioned above, Dr. John Stubbs, who was SFU president in the mid 1990s, reported that all "sense of community just withered" evenings and weekends.

> "We literally walk our girls through the forest to drop them off at school. And I walk right past the grocery store on my way home from the bus. Even on the coldest, rainiest night, we would never think about driving to any of these amenities."

JASON WEGMAN, UNIVERCITY RESIDENT

Few people had a better position from which to watch the transition than Dr. Michael Stevenson, who was SFU president from 2000 to 2010. Not only did he throw his considerable influence behind the project, giving it life at a crucial time, but he and his wife, Jan Whitford, also helped design a new President's Residence in the first major project in the new community, One University Crescent. "I embraced the concept of living there and moved into the first building. It was spectacular, and very useful to me and a tremendous value to the university. I wanted to identify with the university in a direct way and wanted to reinforce the idea of a residential community, to show it as a strategic priority for me." He did so, in part, by creating a space that was appropriate for entertaining visitors, one that would show the university and its breathtaking location in the best light. And it worked: "It was a big surprise for the grandees of Vancouver to be invited up and find that there was a lot going on," Stevenson says.

Of course, there was not a lot going on in the early days. Gabor Vasarhelyi fell in love with the idea of UniverCity in 2003 while he was helping design the stormwater management system as an engineer with CH2M, and he moved to the mountain in 2005 from a Vancouver condo on Beach Avenue facing English Bay. And, in those first days, he admits to having doubted his good judgment. "In the beginning, people shied away from such a unique location," Vasarhelyi says, adding that, after the convenience of living in Vancouver's full-service West End, in the days before the opening of the grocery store, it was a bit of a shock to have to leave the mountain to fetch so much as a bottle of milk.

Jason Wegman arrived in 2006, from Toronto, and bought a two-bedroom townhome in the Serenity project. After the big, flat, eastern capital, Burnaby Mountain was rugged and beautiful and, relative to the choices, a perfectly acceptable one-hour transit commute to his job at PWL Partnership Landscape Architecture in downtown Vancouver. At the time, he wasn't aware the PWL principal Margot Long was already deeply engaged on the mountain or that, soon he would be as well. The early relative isolation was no real issue for him. Wegman says he was too busy running the trails in the Burnaby Mountain Conservation Area. But with the arrival of children (daughters born in 2007 and 2009) and the sort of services that a young family needs (the childcare centre and, in 2010, the elementary school and the full-service grocery store), he found himself completely convinced of his own landscape-architect narrative: people and communities both thrive when everything is well-designed and close enough to be reached conveniently on foot. "We literally walk our girls through the forest to drop them off at school. And I walk right

123

124

UniverCity resident Jason Wegman playing
with his family at Richard Bolton Park.

> "I'm a city guy, and I miss Toronto, the cultural aspects and the diversity. But I can't live there any more. Now, with children, it's all about community."

**YUSUF VARACHIA, UNIVERCITY RESIDENT &
DIRECTOR OF INTERNATIONAL STRATEGIC INITIATIVES, SFU**

past the grocery store on my way home from the bus. Even on the coldest, rainiest night, we would never think about driving to any of these amenities." On the contrary, if it's raining really hard, he pops out to see how the rain gardens and infiltration galleries are performing because, now, UniverCity is part of his job, as well.

Christine Kim and Yusuf Varachia also came to UniverCity from Toronto, urbanite residents of that city's Queen's Quay. Kim signed on in 2007 as a professor in the SFU English department so they grabbed a rental unit in the Verdant building as a place from which to explore the region for a place where they would like to settle down. Daughter Zahra was about 18 months old when they arrived and Kim says they were lucky that her mother was able to come live with them for the first year to look after the baby. Absent a childcare option on the mountain, however, they would have moved off in short order. But in 2008, they got a spot on SFU's established childcare on the west side of the Burnaby Mountain campus and they bought a unit in Verdant, affordable, in part, because of the original Trust/Vancity arrangement to build and sell units for SFU staff and faculty for 20 percent below market value and to protect that better-than-market status for all subsequent buyers. After another baby, Zidan, arrived four years later, for whom they found a childcare space in UniverCity, they were fully committed to UniverCity and traded up to a larger, townhouse unit in Serenity, one of the first consciously family-oriented projects in the early phase of UniverCity's development.

Varachia, who commuted at first to a job as a student recruiter at UBC, says, "I'm a city guy, and I miss Toronto, the cultural aspects and the diversity. But I can't live there any more. Now, with children, it's all about community." He has since taken a job at SFU, where he is now the Director of International

Strategic Initiatives, which means he can get to work in five minutes and, many days, have lunch with Kim. They still have a car, which Kim calls "the world's most expensive grocery cart." On which subject, she says, "When the grocery store came (in 2010), it was really exciting — and a number of people cheered (in 2016) when the liquor store opened up, as well!"

For the Wegmans and the Kim-Varachias, it is all about community, about living in a place where you know your neighbours well. "The neighbours watch each other's children and we know everyone. It's such a tight-knit community, it's like having a ready-made family," Varachia says, adding, "... and when the city beckons, Granville Island is only 35 minutes away."

All together, that may explain why the biannual community survey conducted by The Mustel Group in 2016 found that 91 percent of residents say they would recommend UniverCity to friends and family.

The other big beneficiaries of the UniverCity development are SFU's students in residences. No longer stranded during evenings and weekends, they have the facilities and distractions of the university itself and the services and entertainments of an adjacent, growing and vibrant village.

REFLECTION: *What Works; and What Can We Make Better?*

126

University High Street
and the Lift building.

4: THE NEXT CHAPTER

A Complete Community Takes Flight

It is standard practice in the development industry to work toward the day when you can walk away. Developers and development managers typically spend years on a major project, finding land, assessing its potential, roughing in the designs, working with regulatory officials and neighbours to confirm highest and best use, securing funding, commissioning the work, and then watching like a hawk, or a panicky parent, to encourage what's going right and fix what's going wrong. On the final (one hopes, fabulous) day, you get to snip the ribbon, hand over the keys and, if things have gone well, carry a cheque to the bank. That handover, however, comes with complications. If the project was a single building, you have to ensure that it is fully functional, that the new owners know how to find the fuse boxes and maintain the major systems. You generally — legally — have to leave behind a forwarding address, so everyone knows where to find you if they need your help, or want compensation if things go wrong. This transition is tricky, but it's well-travelled ground; any development industry veteran can tell you the steps.

That's not the case at UniverCity. The complexities multiply immeasurably when you are planning to hand over an entire community, especially one that includes so many features that are innovative or experimental. Indeed, the City of Burnaby allowed UniverCity so much latitude in designing state-of-the-art stormwater management systems or programming one of the narrowest new streets in the region, and maybe in the country (The Mews), entirely because SFU Community Trust was going to continue acting as the master plan development manager. Burnaby's stated position was that the City would accept final responsibility for these features only if the Trust could demonstrate, to its satisfaction, that everything is working and will be no more difficult or expensive to maintain than a conventional subdivision.

The impending handover is further complicated because a significant amount of the infrastructure and some major real estate assets are going to remain in the active control of our only shareholder, Simon Fraser University. For example, there are commercial and residential buildings that will bring the university revenue in perpetuity but need to be managed over that same, endless time span. The Trust must ensure that these assets will arrive as a gift, not a liability.

Then there are the residents of UniverCity, including a majority of owners who have bet with their life savings that this new community will be sustainable, at the very least, for them. Community sustainability is about so much more than energy efficiency and service reliability. It's about safety and security. It's about liveability. It's about common commitment to rules

> Community sustainability is about so much more than energy efficiency and service reliability. It's about safety and security. It's about liveability. It's about common commitment to rules that are easy to follow and easier to keep people to. It's about forging relationships among neighbours and between residents and businesses and, in this community, between town and gown.

that are easy to follow and easier to keep people to. It's about forging relationships among neighbours and between residents and businesses and, in this community, between town and gown. The community and the university have so much potential to be a benefit to one another, but as the residents of any university town will tell you, there are also potential tensions. So, before we even contemplate closing up shop, SFU Community Trust has to consider everything from mitigating the noise to manicuring the greenery.

That's just what we are doing. Even as we manage an accelerating development calendar (we're barely a year away from leasing our last development parcel), we are assembling an "Owner's Manual"

128

Lift and the Slopes Mews.

129

that will give full confidence to the City of Burnaby, the University and the neighbours that we, at the Trust, are entirely dispensable, and that the whole of UniverCity will continue to flourish — and perhaps to expand — even after we have departed.

If the notion of expansion rings like a potential negative, it shouldn't. There is room, physically, and there is space in the City of Burnaby's development allotment, because in one regard we have overachieved, dramatically.

To meet the definition of "sustainable," a community must be more than environmentally robust; it must also be economically viable.

The narrative by which we have guided our actions, and the one that we have shared with the world, including from the earliest pages of this book, is that Simon Fraser University began with 385 hectares, but satisfied itself with developing only 65, dedicating the remaining property for permanent preservation within the Burnaby Mountain Conservation Area. We did this to limit our footprint on the land, and to build a community that was truly pedestrian-oriented, one in which residents can reach all the services and transportation linkages they need within a walk of less than 10 minutes. In the process, however, we didn't actually develop 65 hectares. UniverCity's current footprint is barely one-third of that. Even accommodating the permanent protection of an expanded Naheeno Park inside the university ring road, there are still two large parcels within our allowable development area.

One of those parcels might never be developed. The "South Neighbourhood," which straddles Naheeno Park on the eastern portion of the property, sits on a steep, wet slope immediately below the university. Even aside from the environmental complications, it's possible that the daunting costs of engineering and water management will mean that the land remains economically unsuitable for development. The western portion of the "South Neighbourhood," lying southwest of the campus, would be more easily developed from a geotechnical perspective. But it is well outside a 10-minute walking range from the rest of the UniverCity community. It may, in the future, be deemed appropriate for university use, or perhaps SFU could negotiate to exchange some of that parcel for the northern-most section of Naheeno Park — the piece that is directly adjacent the university. But it seems unlikely that the "southwest" neighbourhood will ever fit into the compact and walkable community of UniverCity. A third, small "Swing Area" on the eastern edge of the undeveloped parcel is also steep and wet. We have considered it as a reasonable addition to the Conservation Area, though not formally.

Having removed these parcels from the mix, we find ourselves falling short of the number of units that the City of Burnaby agreed could be developed within the university ring road. This could be considered both a disappointment and a problem. It's disappointing because one of the Trust's mandates is to earn revenue for the teaching and research mission of SFU. We certainly have fulfilled that mandate. Calculating the likely income of all the projects that are in the ground or on the drawing board, we estimate that we will leave SFU with an endowment in the $90-million range. But we also know what good use Canada's premier comprehensive university can make of endowment income; it seems wrong not to do all that we can.

More critically, however, the target population of 10,000 was no accident and missing the target could come at a cost. One of the great advantages that SFU Community Trust has enjoyed from the outset was the expertise of a blue-chip board of directors; we have had consistent guidance from some of the most experienced and knowledgeable people in the Vancouver development community. They, in turn, calculated the optimal number of residents that would be necessary to support the range of commercial, educational and social services required in a functional, sustainable, liveable community that is somewhat isolated from the surrounding metropolis. As mentioned earlier, the Trust considered it a prudent and necessary investment to subsidize certain commercial tenants while the community was still developing, the grocery store, for example. It was important to give everyone a chance to establish themselves while the population was building up to a critical mass. But it's in no one's interest to have to maintain subsidies beyond a certain point. To meet the definition of "sustainable," a community must be more than environmentally robust; it must also be economically viable. So, we continue to look for development opportunities that will allow us to complement the community and support the university.

UniverCity community residents.

131

THE NEXT CHAPTER: *A Complete Community Takes Flight*

MONITOR, MEASURE, AND RECALIBRATE

The only way to ever really know if something has worked well is to go back and check: to monitor, to measure, to ask for feedback and to listen. Then, if things have not turned out as you had hoped, you can adjust. And even if it is something you cannot undo, at least you can avoid doing it again.

This is the essence of continuous improvement, a way to maximize your opportunity to get the most out of your project — and to make sure that you get good references.

In development, it can mean checking everything from water and energy consumption to the state and volume of sewage outflow. It can mean counting cars in the parking lots or strollers on the sidewalk. It inevitably means checking with the people who now use your creation, however big and however complex, to find out what they like and what they hope you can do better.

So, check, constantly. You might not always record a big success. But it will give you one more chance to fend off failure, and sometimes, that may be your biggest win.

132

Community members at the
Naheeno Park Community Garden.

UniverCityNews
THE COMMUNITY AT SIMON FRASER

Number 03 • Summer 2005

Charter Residents Move In

A few of the first residents gather for a community photo.

Another New Beginning

TOP LEFT: UniverCity Charter residents How Yin and Elsie Leung.

TOP RIGHT: Front page of the community newsletter featuring some charter residents.

BOTTOM: Residents gather in the Town Square for a Community Celebration, 2006.

OPPOSITE, TOP: Celebrating the community's five-year anniversary.

OPPOSITE, BOTTOM: UniverCity residents commemorate the community's ten year anniversary with pancakes and a celebration photo.

BUILDING COMMUNITY: *Defining, Designing, Developing UniverCity*

THE NEXT CHAPTER: *A Complete Community Takes Flight*

136

Dale Mikkelsen and Nancy Spooner on a walk-about through the community.

Crisis Communications: The Plan You Can't Live Without

Imagine the worst thing that could happen — and then consider that a crisis, by nature, is worse than you can imagine.

That was the excellent advice that SFU Community Trust received almost a decade ago from our invaluable communications advisor, Nancy Spooner. In a fascinating career, Spooner has been involved in the management or review of crises ranging from food poisonings at an organic food restaurant to the bombing of the Boston Marathon. And she says that, in debriefs, everyone acknowledges the same overarching problem: communications.

"Most organizations have a formal Crisis Management Plan, which is an operations plan," Spooner says. "It's all about how to minimize damage to the asset." But what happens when the asset is your reputation, or if the safety of those on or near your premises is at stake and you haven't got a plan to communicate with them? What happens when reporters start showing up? When do you speak? Who speaks? Who do you call (in your organization and your community)? Who makes the calls? There is no time to ponder any of these decisions in the midst of an actual crisis.

So, however big your organization is, you need a plan, whether the main subjects turn out to be managerial (sexual harassment), financial (fraud, bankruptcy), technological (I.T. failure from hacking or viruses), natural disasters, or crimes and terrorism.

You need to identify stakeholders, assess risk, and sort potential crises into three levels:

1. No media contact necessary, little likelihood of lasting reputational damage;

2. Likely provoking media interest or a reasonable call for accountability, raising long-term reputational risk, and demanding a partial call-out of crisis team;

3. All hands on deck!

Then you need to identify "all hands" — a well-prepared team, all of whom have a short, grab-and-go plan, with contact lists loaded in their phones (and recorded in hardcopy for backup).

By good fortune, UniverCity has had only one occasion to trigger our plan, which worked perfectly in a Level One incident that could easily have escalated, otherwise.

Two final cautions: First, your crisis communications plan is likely to trigger a planning cascade, as you realize how unprepared you are on other counts.

Second, every plan needs to be updated at least annually. Contact lists are only useful when they are fresh.

The most tempting of these opportunities lies right outside the window of the Trust offices. It's the East Parking lot, a large paved surface immediately south of The Cornerstone and Hub buildings, which are functionally the commercial centre of UniverCity and the principal connection point between SFU and the community. The East Parking lot is reasonably well used; a number of students and faculty still commute to the campus daily in private automobiles. But auto usage is in decline, and is likely to fall farther, faster when the aerial transit link goes into operation. And, in any case,

a new, smaller East lot development could include an adequate amount of replacement structured parking spaces.

The potential at this site is fabulous. As designed, the transit link will land on Burnaby Mountain just south of the Town Square between SFU and UniverCity and right beside the East Parking lot. This link will become SFU's front door, a meeting and greeting place and the perfect interface for SFU, UniverCity, tourists and other users. SFU's Strategic Vision is to be "Canada's most community-

Friends in front of the CentreBlock building.

One of the great ambitions for UniverCity is that it might be a model of sustainable planning and practice.

research facilities in Discovery Park. And to the southeast, it might step down to meet the lower-density, larger-unit, family-oriented neighbourhood now developing in the Slopes neighbourhood.

The site demands an ambitious plan. It is too valuable to the university and the community to be programmed hurriedly or without significant investment from various levels of government. We might begin with an early commitment to the aerial transit link, which will make a huge contribution to the sustainability of the community (and make transit service more reliable and robust) and to the quality of life of students, staff, faculty and residents who commute on and off the mountain every day. The gondola service would enhance, immeasurably, the accessibility and significance of this location.

You can, perhaps, understand a degree of ambivalence in the SFU Community Trust offices: it is against a flurry of excitement about the future that we contemplate winding down our operations. A shrinking staff is working feverishly, enthusiastically and with an ever-increasing sense of accomplishment toward a day, within the next five years, when we will say goodbye. We will leave with a deep sense of gratitude and a warm sense of optimism, not just that UniverCity will remain one of the most sustainable urban communities on earth, but that it will also be self-sustaining, that it will have critical mass, and that its low-carbon, low-impact operations will continue long into the future.

Finally, we hope that others will find a way to share our successes (and learn from our mistakes). One of the great ambitions for UniverCity is that it might be a model of sustainable planning and practice. The Trust staff has been grateful for the leadership shown by SFU and the support, encouragement, and guidance that we received from the City of Burnaby, and from our Board of Directors. We hope that UniverCity will continue to provide insight into how best to develop a compact, walkable, liveable and sustainable urban community, long after we at SFU Community Trust have fulfilled our mandate and passed on the baton.

engaged research university." A well-designed gateway on the East lot could be a purpose-built point of engagement, including the first mixed-use building on the mountain that freely integrates university and community activities and populations. It would be a logical location for university admissions and tours, and a perfect place for a conference facility, perhaps sharing services with a boutique hotel in the upper storeys to accommodate short-term visitors to the university or the community. On the north edge of the building, it might make sense to carry on the small-scale retail/commercial presence and townhomes along The Mews, creating a busy, pedestrian-friendly edge to match the vitality on the existing north side. Upper floors might include office space, with condo or rental residential above. On the southern edge, the development could link to the commercial laboratories and other

138

Rendering of the proposed gondola travelling from the Production Way skytrain station to the Town Square at UniverCity.

139

Rendering of the proposed SFU East Gateway project at the western edge of UniverCity, where the community meets the campus. The project encompasses a future gondola landing, Parcel 24 building in the High Street neighbourhood, and the integration of the East Campus Road bus station.

141

THE NEXT CHAPTER: *A Complete Community Takes Flight*

AWARDS & RECOGNITION

UniverCity's winning reputation attracts national and international media attention, including coverage in *BC Business Magazine, Granville Magazine, Vancouver Magazine, Shared Vision, Sunday New York Times, Maclean's Magazine, Grist Magazine, Dialogue Magazine, Business in Vancouver Green Edition, the Toronto Star,* and *the Vancouver Province and Sun.*

David Suzuki's television program the Nature of Things highlighted UniverCity as a healthy, walkable community on 'The Weight of the World', as did Metro Vancouver on their program 'Our Livable Region'.

UniverCity is also often featured as a leader in sustainable development at workshops and conferences across Canada, the United States, and beyond.

AMERICAN PLANNING ASSOCIATION – National Excellence Award for Innovation in Green Community Planning

ASSOCIATION OF UNIVERSITY REAL ESTATE OFFICIALS (AUREO) – Award of Excellence

BC HYDRO POWER SMART EXCELLENCE AWARD – Residential Building Developer for The Cornerstone

BURNABY BOARD OF TRADE – Newsmaker of the Year Award

CANADA GREEN BUILDING COUNCIL (CAGBC) NATIONAL LEADERSHIP AWARDS – Green Building Champion Award (UniverCity Childcare Centre)

CANADIAN HOME BUILDERS' ASSOCIATION – SAM Award for Best Community Development in Canada

CANADIAN HOME BUILDERS' ASSOCIATION – Georgie Award to The Cornerstone for Best Environmental Consideration and Energy Efficiency

CANADIAN INSTITUTE OF PLANNERS – Award for Planning Excellence: Neighbourhood Planning

CANADIAN MORTGAGE AND HOUSING CORPORATION (CMHC) – Best Practices in Affordable Housing Award for the Verdant @ UniverCity

CANADIAN SOCIETY LANDSCAPE ARCHITECTS – Award of Excellence for the UniverCity Childcare Centre

CITY OF BURNABY – Environment Award Planning and Development for Phase 4 of the UniverCity Masterplan

CITY OF BURNABY – Environment Award for Planning and Development for The Cornerstone

CITY OF BURNABY – Environment Award Planning and Development for the UniverCity Childcare Centre

CITY OF BURNABY – Environment Award for Planning and Development for the Verdant @ UniverCity

FEDERATION OF CANADIAN MUNICIPALITIES – Sustainable Communities Award for Integrated Neighbourhood Development

FORTISBC – Award for Excellence in Energy Efficiency in New Construction for Origin

GREATER VANCOUVER HOME BUILDERS' ASSOCIATION – Ovation Award Excellence in Energy Efficiency in New Construction: Multi-Family for Origin

GREATER VANCOUVER HOME BUILDERS' ASSOCIATION – Ovation Award Best Multi-Family Lowrise Development for Origin

INTERNATIONAL LIVING FUTURE INSTITUTE - Living Building Hero Award

LIVCOM AWARDS – Gold Award and third place-ranking overall in the Sustainable Projects Category

PLANNING INSTITUTE OF BRITISH COLUMBIA – Award of Excellence for Site Planning and Design

PLANNING INSTITUTE OF BRITISH COLUMBIA – Award of Excellence for UniverCity Phase 3 Masterplan & Zoning

QUALITY URBAN ENERGY SYSTEMS OF TOMORROW - QUEST Community Energy Builder Award

URBAN DEVELOPMENT INSTITUTE – Award for Excellence in Urban Development Best Sustainable for UniverCity Childcare Centre

URBAN DEVELOPMENT INSTITUTE – Award for Innovations in Creating a More Livable & Sustainable Region

URBAN DEVELOPMENT INSTITUTE – Award to the Verdant @ UniverCity for Innovations in Creating More Affordable Housing

URBAN DEVELOPMENT INSTITUTE – Award to the Verdant @ UniverCity for Innovations in Creating More Sustainable Development

URBAN DEVELOPMENT INSTITUTE – Award for Excellence in Urban Development for the Cornerstone

URBAN LAND INSTITUTE – Award for Excellence: The Americas for Best Practice in Design, Architecture and Development

VANCOUVER REGIONAL CONSTRUCTION ASSOCIATION – Silver Award of Excellence Sustainable Construction category for the UniverCity Childcare Centre

TOOLS, RESOURCES & SUGGESTED READINGS

PUBLICATIONS

*Radical Campus:
Making Simon Fraser University*
by Hugh Johnson
Douglas & McIntyre, 2005

*A Pattern Language:
Towns, Buildings, Construction*
by Christopher Alexander,
Sara Ishikawa, and Murray Silverstein
Oxford University Press, 1977

Arthur Erickson: An Architect's Life
by David Stouck
Douglas & McIntyre, 2013

Towards Sustainable Communities
by Dr. Mark Roseland
New Society Publishers, 2012

Living Building Challenge 3.1
International Living Future Institute

Living Community Challenge 1.2
International Living Future Institute

*Generation Green: The Making of
the UniverCity Childcare Centre*
by Michael D. Berrisford
Ecotone Publishing, 2014

UniverCity ARTWalk
by SFU Community Trust,
2014

*Two Trees: a celebration of art,
ecology and community*
by SFU Community Trust
Simon Fraser University Reprographics,
2005

WEBSITES

UniverCity:
www.UniverCity.ca

SFU Community Trust
Green Building Guidelines:
www.univercity.ca/planning-development

UniverCity ARTWalk:
www.univercity.ca/culture-events/
univercity-artwalk

UniverCity community biannual survey:
www.univercity.ca/media/research

International Living Future Institute:
https://living-future.org

PHOTOS & ILLUSTRATIONS

Front Cover: The Hub building
Photo: Derek Lepper Photography

Back Cover Author Photo:
Peppa Martin - Truth and Beauty Studio

**All photos by SFU Creative Services
except as noted:**

Andy Gavel: page 139

Anita Alberto Photography: page 134, 135

Arthur Erickson and Herb Auerbach:
pages 26, 27

CH2M Hill: page 62

Corix Multi-Utility Services: page 83

Dale Mikkelsen: page 99

Derek Lepper Photography: page 87

Écho-logis: page 76

George Allen: page 21

Hendrickson Photography:
pages 28, 114, 131

Hoots Inc.: page 78

Hotson Bakker Architects (Dialog):
pages 13, 35, 52

Hughes Condon Marler Architects:
page 73

Jesse Galicz: page 51

Kaylin Co: page 92

Martin Tessler: pages 70, 75, 84, 91, 120

Moodie Consultants Ltd.: page 31

Pansy Hui: pages 81, 112

Paul Nowarre: page 10

Peppa Martin - Truth and Beauty Studio:
pages 8, 37, 46, 98, 102, 131, 135, 138

Perkins + Will: page 140

Porte Communities: page 100

Shutterstock: pages 16, 23

Schmittenhöhebahn/Johannes Felsch:
page 45

SFU Community Trust: pages 135, 138

SITE Photography:
pages 88, 116, 117, 118, 119, 126

INTERNATIONAL
LIVING FUTURE
INSTITUTE℠

INTERNATIONAL LIVING FUTURE INSTITUTE

The International Living Future Institute (ILFI) is a hub for visionary programs. ILFI offers global strategies for lasting sustainability, partnering with local communities to create grounded and relevant solutions, including green building and infrastructure solutions on scales ranging from single room renovations to neighborhoods or whole cities. ILFI administers the Living Building Challenge and the Living Community Challenge, the built environment's most rigorous and ambitious performance standards. It is the parent organization for Cascadia Green Building Council, a chapter of both the United States and Canada Green Building Councils that serves Alaska, British Columbia, Washington and Oregon. It is also home to Ecotone Publishing, a unique publishing house dedicated to telling the story of the green building movement's pioneering thinkers and practitioners.

LIVING BUILDING CHALLENGE

The Living Building Challenge is the built environment's most rigorous performance standard. It calls for the creation of building projects at all scales that operate as cleanly, beautifully, and efficiently as nature's architecture. To be certified under the Challenge, projects must meet a series of ambitious performance requirements, including net zero energy, waste, and water, over a minimum of twelve months of continuous occupancy.

LIVING COMMUNITY CHALLENGE

The Living Community Challenge is a framework for master planning, design, and construction. It is a tool to create a symbiotic relationship between people and all aspects of the built environment. The program is a call to action to governments, campuses, planners, developers and neighborhood groups to create communities that are as connected and beautiful as a forest.

ECOTONE PUBLISHING

Founded by green building experts in 2004, Ecotone Publishing is dedicated to meeting the growing demand for authoritative and accessible books on sustainable design, materials selection and building techniques in North America and beyond. Ecotone searches out and documents inspiring projects, visionary people, and innovative trends that are leading the design industry to transformational change toward a healthier planet.